Who Speaks For the Children?

GIVING VOICE TO A FORGOTTEN GENERATION

PETER SILVERMAN

Stoddart

Published in 1989 by
Stoddart Publishing Co. Limited
34 Lesmill Road
Toronto, Ontario
M3B 2T6

Canadian Cataloguing in Publication Data

Silverman, Peter
Who speaks for the children?

Rev. ed.
Includes bibliographical references.
ISBN 0-7737-5257-9

1. Child Welfare - Canada
2. Child Abuse - Canada
I. Title.

HV745.A6S5 1989   362.7'044   C89-093331-6

Cover design by Brant Cowie/Artplus
Printed in Canada by Gagné Printing Ltd.

*To my daughters, Alexis and Leah,
because they have lived in love
and have come to know the joy of life.
And to "Smurf" and "Mouse,"
who still have the courage
to seek love.*

Contents

Preface

A decade ago, *Who Speaks for the Children?* was published in its first edition. The book emerged out of my anger after I had reported on the inquest into the death of one-month-old Vicky Starr Ellis, a child who, as I wrote at the time, was doomed to die. As the five-week inquest in Toronto dragged on through June and July of 1977, it became apparent that Vicky died because of gross failures in the child welfare system. Doctors, children's aid societies and social workers of all descriptions failed to save the child from her parents, Deborah and Brooks Ellis. Vicky was Deborah's fifth child, and the third to die. One child, Charlene, died of neglect, according to a coroner's inquest; another drowned while unattended in a bathtub. Said Dr. Elly Cass, who ordered and conducted the inquest into Vicky's death, ''Deborah's track record as a mother left a lot to be desired.''

All the children, including Vicky, had been or were in the care of the children's aid society. Deborah Ellis had a two-foot-thick dossier, which contained warnings from judges and social workers that ''she was a danger to any children she may have.'' This was the opinion also of Judge S.G. Tinker, who heard the charges of criminal neglect against Deborah, who was accused of ''not providing the necessities of life'' for her second daughter, Darlene. The coroner's jury, which inquired into the death of Darlene, said, "The various authorities should not lose sight of the fact that their prime concern is the welfare of the surviving child, Charlene." Charlene did survive, and so did Brooks, Jr. He was made a Crown ward by Judge Norris Weisman, who acted on the advice of the assistant director of the family court clinic of the Clarke Institute of Psychiatry, Ruth Parry.

That was January 19, 1977. Less than a month later, on February 9, 1977, the same judge awarded Vicky back to her parents, again on the advice of Ruth Parry, whose impassioned testimony — forty-three pages of it — swept all before it. "Since part of Mrs. Ellis's personality disorder was a compulsion to have children," she told the court, "and since nothing could be done to prevent it, she should have another chance, through Vicky, to learn how to mother for the sake of children yet unborn." Vicky would be therapy for her mother. According to Judge Weisman, Ruth Parry was "repeatedly asked whether, in light of past events, there was any danger in returning the child to Mrs. Ellis. In her opinion, there was no immediate risk to the baby that would warrant exclusion from its parents." No one was in court to argue for Vicky. The battle was between the children's aid society and Deborah and Brooks Ellis.

Three weeks later, on March 2, at 10:03 in the evening, Vicky Starr Ellis was pronounced dead. For twelve hours the staff at Toronto's Hospital for Sick Children had fought to save the child's life. In his report, pathologist Dr. D. Fagin wrote that while he could not precisely state the cause of death, Vicky had probably died of swelling of the brain brought on by improper feeding of a high-sodium-level baby formula. In addition, the child suffered from severe electrolyte imbalance, gastroenteritis and high body-fluid loss due to explosive diarrhea. The coroner's jury recommended that any more children Deborah Ellis had be immediately seized by the children's aid society. That recommendation was carried out.

My anger during that inquest prompted me to write a book about the child welfare system and its weaknesses. I wanted to find out how the system had failed to protect Vicky from her parents, and from death. At the end of the book I wrote that, as far as protecting children is concerned, "The record shows that we do not yet care enough."

Now, ten years later, my publisher has asked me to have another look, to determine if anything at all has changed in the decade that has passed. Was that final sentence still the summary of child protection in Canada? This book is the result. It is not a definitive study of child welfare. That I leave to others, many of whom kindly helped me with this book. They are far better equipped to deal with the workings of the child welfare system than I am. Instead, this book looks at the system through the eyes of those who are in it: provincial court judges, child welfare workers, foster parents, governments, lawyers and police — and the kids. I interviewed people across Canada to hear their reflections and feelings about the problem, the system and its functioning. Listening to them led me to a bitter conclusion: for too many of our children, even a little bit of love is too expensive.

As I said in the preface of the first book: there are no villains, just people trying as best they can to protect and succor our kids. Many gave unstintingly of their time in answering my questions. With a few exceptions, all were brutally frank.

Writing a book like this is a partnership between the author, the editor and the publisher. It also involves others, like my wife, who took up the initial burden of looking over the rough draft and suggesting changes — for the better. My two daughters showed me the other side of a child's life, that it can be loving and without fear and pain.

There are those who gave their time, who had to put up with the author, clutching tape recorder and note-pad, armed with a seemingly endless list of questions that would try the patience of Job, let alone a harried social worker. Then there were the nights I spent in doughnut shops, or walking the track, or listening to odd conversations at hours when most of the city is asleep, no tape recorders now, no questions, just eyes and ears. People who work the streets are a skittish lot, both the hunter and the hunted. The sidewalks and alleys are both friend and enemy, and strange faces are seldom trusted. The discussions around tables were easier, with kids who have been through the system or worked the streets and are willing to tell their experiences. These I met through welfare agencies, social workers, friends. Then the tape recorder worked, endlessly recording their lives. Looking back, one could say this book is a product of the electronic age, not only tape recorders and television clips, but the telephone, which allowed me to reach across the country and extend my persistent questioning from Vancouver to St. John's.

But of course none of this would have been possible without the willingness of dozens of people, from street kids to child welfare workers to teachers, to succumb to my prying and probing. I owe them a debt, and I hope this book repays it, in part. I realize this debt as

I look down at a large cardboard box, containing a hundred tapes, each at least two hours long, all those hours a small part of other people's time and energy. There is no other way; there are no shortcuts. In the end it was my task to reduce the mass to some form and substance and my editor, Edna Barker, could then step in and make sure there was not only substance, but style.

Many of those I interviewed asked to remain anonymous. Some feared their position could be jeopardized; others feared that publicity would make it difficult to work with clients and colleagues. I would like to thank them, as well as others who helped make this book possible: Barbara Chisholm, Dr. Herb Sohn, the York Region Family and Children's Services, Mary McKin, John Meston, Justice for Children, Mary Bogue, Ken Shaw, the National Youth in Care Network, Peter Fraser, Senior Judge Lucien Beaulieu, John Jagt, Valerie Scovill, Corinne Robertshaw, Jamie Martin, Gary Lack, Beth Joseph, Sharon Richards, John Turvey, Professor Marlyn Callahan, Professor Bernard Dickens, Nancy French, Fay Martin, Lonny Mark, Kate Watt, Covenant House, Lorna Grant, Brenda Rau, Chris Walmsey, Maureen Duffy, the Canadian Child Welfare Association, the Pape Adolescent Center, Sheila Williams, Professor Chris Bagley, Mary McCovelle, Heather Sprould, Judge James Nevins, Holly Henderson, Professor Andrew Armitage, Judge Peter Leveque, Allison Burnett, Connie Snow, Marilyn McCormack, Ruth Heron, Saen Pryke, Kimberley Smith, Martin Zakrajsek, Susanne Hamilton, and Jacqueline Lewis.

I would like to express my appreciation to the York Region Family and Children's Services for their help, and for patiently answering my endless calls for information. I owe a debt to Covenant House, and to the Pape Avenue Adolescent Resource Centre, who kindly allowed me interview their clients. And to those street kids, the kids I met at odd hours, in bars, doughnut shops, on street corners, in alleys and restaurants, and to the other kids, those in care or just out of it, who have been through the system — thanks for the insights into your lives.

Finally, I would never have managed to meet the deadline of my patient publisher, Bill Hanna, without the invaluable help of my wife, Professor France (Chesca) Burton, who read the manuscript, corrected and edited it, and at the same time was, as always, a loving mother to our sixteen-year-old twins, Leah and Alexis.

Introduction

A warm Toronto summer evening. The Covenant House vehicle is parked in downtown Toronto. The door opens and two women get out, one white, the other black. By any description, they are very attractive, except one is, in fact, a man; the other is her "friend," her protector. Neither is older than eighteen. They are part of the growing number of street kids that hits Canada's big cities during the summer months. Some are weekend runners, looking for a few kicks and forty-eight hours of freedom before returning to the nice home in the suburbs; others are looking, feeling out the streets, making contacts, perhaps not even knowing why, but sooner or later they, too, will run, and will stay out on the streets. But for now they will return home. Others are not so fortunate. They are here because there are no other options. They are fleeing the violence, the abuse, the alcoholism, the drugs; or they have been thrown out. Whatever the street offers is better than what they left. These kids are the walking wounded of family life in the 1980s. They are the visible results of what too many families are doing to too many kids. Behind them is another army of kids who suffer in silence, who do not run, who suppress the tears, the screams, and just try to survive. They are the emotionally and physically wounded, but no one is hearing the cries for help.

Perhaps it is because we live in an illusion about the family and about children. By the still accepted conventions we are supposed to marry, settle down, have kids, and there is strong pressure to have a career, as well. That's what Hollywood is saying; what television is promoting. The theme of the latest big-selling movie production is that having a baby is fun. Anyone who has children knows that much of it is not fun, that having a child does not turn the parent into a responsible, mature adult. As child welfare expert Barbara Chisholm noted, "Motherhood does not flow with the milk."

Canadians are having kids at the rate of a thousand a day. A thousand sets of parents are suddenly finding responsibility, but not all of them can accept it. We are placing intolerable strains on the family unit. Compared with many third-world societies, which still have large extended families, our civilization, while leaping forward in a technological sense, has gone backward in terms of the family. Job demands, the need for two incomes, population mobility, housing conditions and changing social attitudes have all weakened the family unit. No longer are there aunts, uncles, grandparents and even distant cousins able to advise, counsel and support. Regardless of what the anti-abortion people may say, there are a lot of unwanted kids out there — unwanted now and, in the end, unwanted by anyone. In the end we pay, and pay heavily, with myriad facilities to help children and young adults who are on drugs, are emotionally crippled and are in poor health. They have few skills to get a job; they rely on welfare or crime, from pushing drugs to hooking. A whole child- and young-adult welfare industry has sprung up, from natal health to hostels, to child welfare agencies and social workers, to police juvenile squads. The cost runs into the billions. That's one price. The other is the wasted lives of these kids.

True, we have made some progress. Society has accepted that a child has the right to be fed, housed, clothed and emotionally nurtured. But society has not completed the equation. It has not said just what these obligations mean, nor how they are to be translated into the reality of caring for the child. Perhaps we are still not sure just where the child fits into society. Children are maturing, physically and mentally, so fast that simple authoritarianism doesn't work anymore. Kids are far more ready to challenge parental authority. Parents use force or economic pressure to control their children. Yet while parents must cope with their rapidly maturing kids, the kids are remaining dependent for longer periods of time. From the moment the child is born, he or she becomes the consumer of the parents' emotional, physical and economic resources. Too often, a family will not have enough resources to cope. That is when things start to fall apart. There is an anomaly here. Dependency leads to inferior status, a lack of say in how the child should be treated and in how the parents' obligations will be carried out. Two hundred years ago, the great English jurist William Blackstone outlined the legal dimensions of parenthood. He established that children had duties to their families, while parents had rights over their children. Today, regardless of the Canadian Charter of Rights, society still thinks of children as chattels— passive, dependent and largely incompetent.

While parents still exercise considerable rights over their children, many of those rights and responsibilities are being shifted to the state. Allowances for the family and single mothers, free education, medical care and child welfare agencies are accepted as obligations of the government.

The position of children was summed up by Joseph Goldstein, Anna Freud and Albert Solnit in their book *Before the Best Interests of the Child.*[1] They point out that the child is singled out by law, as by custom (at least in modern times), for special attention, and is distinguished from adults in physical, psychological and social terms. Adults are recognized by law as responsible for themselves, able to make decisions in their own interests. Children are not so regarded. They are dependent and in need of continuous care by adults who are committed, as parents, to assume that responsibility. Parents, therefore, have obligations toward their children, and those obligations are sanctioned by law. But children have no right to demand anything from their parents. They must rely on the good faith of adults and the law to protect them, but the law only intervenes when the parents have failed. Children are a minority, but they have no access to redress for discrimination or abuse. Not for them human rights commissions or protection under the laws against discrimination. It is not numbers that count. It is strength and power, and kids have little of either.

What happens when adults do not carry out their obligations? What happens when the interests of the parents conflict with the best interests of the child? When should the state intervene? And once it intervenes, who protects the protected from the protectors? Note that whenever there is conflict between a child and an adult, the first assumption is that the child is at fault. R.D. Laing, a world authority in the field of family relations, tells a story from 1860 about a boy who hated his father; a psychiatrist, a certain Professor Morel, was asked to intervene. The good professor immediately asked how it was possible that the boy could hate his father. Clearly there was nothing the matter with the father, a good man, a respected member of society. How was one to reconcile the child's hatred with the father's public image? Clearly there must be something wrong with the boy. He was deemed to need immediate treatment, and was duly sent to an institution. An attempt was made to understand the boy's behavior by examining his head or his psyche, carefully avoiding any examination of the family or the father. Laing wrote, "People have been examining the heads, blood and urine or the psychopathology of such boys and girls ever since."[2]

It is not surprising that the image of the child protectors leaves much to be desired. The middle class sees the child welfare agencies as doing a competent job. But low-income families, the families who deal with the agencies, regard them with fear and mistrust. The agencies are perceived as having great authority. After all, they have the power to remove the child, and some agencies exercise that power without regard for people's rights.

How will the child welfare agencies reconcile their mandate to preserve the family, to work with the parents, with their need to protect the child? Sometimes the child gets lost in the shuffle. "Preserve the family" has indeed become the motto of child welfare agencies across the nation. Cynics say this is because it's cheaper to leave the kids at home than to provide the proper facilities for them. Others say that taking children away is often worse than leaving them at home: they invoke the old adage that the cure is worse than the disease.

The truth is in between. Removing the children is a last resort. Yet after the kids have been removed, there are no resources to meet their needs. Child-care workers know this. One of them explained, ''We sometimes gamble that we can help the family and leave the child at home. But God help us if we screw up.'' Certainly society won't forgive them if they screw up. The workers will be fired. Will society then provide the money to alter the situation? No.

Twenty years ago, R.D. Laing commented on the relations between the child and the family, expectations for children and the conditioning of children:

> We like the food served up elegantly before us: we do not want to know about the animal factories, the slaughterhouses and what goes on in the kitchen. Our own cities are our own animal factories; families, schools, churches are the slaughter-houses of our children; colleges and other places are the kitchens. As adults in marriages and business, we eat the product.[3]

Harsh words, an indictment of what our society does to our children, and not even with evil intent. Frequently the sins are of omission, not commission, the result of ignorance, of strain, of tensions; the beating is done out of love. But too often the evil intent is there, the abuse is deliberate, the pain and suffering are caused with malice aforethought by adults who know the child is unable to retaliate. Society reserves its most severe punishments for those who assault other adults;

it can afford to do so because the incidence of adult assault is far less frequent than the incidence of assaults on children. Children do seem to receive less regard than adults.

Society has accepted that not all is well with children and families, and we have created a complex system of agencies and services designed to deal with the problem. Yet having put the system in place, governments are loath to support them. On too many occasions, the first items on the budget list to be cut are social services. The result is that the system does not work, except in the most basic way. Politicians seem unwilling to accept that it is pay now or pay a lot more later, when the real costs of dealing with present problems concerning child welfare will start to emerge. But then, how many politicians ever plan beyond the next election? The result is that the child welfare mandate, of protection and prevention, becomes instead crisis intervention. The child receives the best that is available — but that is not necessarily what is best for the child.

Yet many would argue, perhaps correctly, that the majority of kids grow up in "normal," reasonably happy homes. These are not the children who come under the scrutiny of the state, its agencies and representatives. The children who do are only a fraction of the victims from those families who abuse their children, but never receive any help or support. Nor do those kids receive any relief from the pain.

ONE

Street Kids

February 12. It's a bitterly cold Toronto winter night. I am in the Covenant House RV, which is operated by two volunteers and two permanent staff. The RV, or van, as the staff call it, cruises the areas where the street kids hang out, the hookers, the transvestites, the gay boys who turn tricks for males. The concept of using a van originated in New York. The van is a mobile refuge where street kids can get a sandwich, some juice or a hot chocolate.

As we move through the night, staff members make sandwiches and get the hot chocolate ready. John O'Byrne is the senior staff member on board. He's got a face that is without illusions or pretense; eyes that have seen it all but have not lost a sense of compassion. His face suggests that some of the seeing was hard indeed. ''We don't preach, we don't lecture and we don't judge. If we can get these kids to come in and have a coffee or a juice, that's fine. If they begin to trust us, perhaps one or two will ask us for help. We tell them the services they can go to, to get off the street. If that happens — and once in a while it does — then this whole exercise is a success.''

The van rolls through the streets and parks at the corner of Queen Street and Triller. One of the volunteers, Bill Purcell, looks out the window. ''There's a sting going down.'' I look out. Jammed into two phone booths are three very large men with toques on, trying to look as if they belong. Across the street, lounging in a beer store, are two more men, while two cars are parked in front of a small strip mall. On the opposite corner, two policewomen try to look like hookers. ''They're too healthy-looking,'' says Bill. ''Too well dressed. One has a fur coat on.'' But the sting works and a john is arrested for trying to hire the ''hooker.''

The next day I listen to taped conversations at Toronto's CITY Pulse News. My colleague, Mark Daily, has been doing a story on the sting operation. On the tapes, the negotiations have a tone of banter; the participants could be bargaining over a rug in a bazaar. But they're bargaining over sex. It's someone's body that's for sale. The voices move from fiscal sparring to hard negotiations. Sex has its own dialogue:

''What do you want?''

''You know what I want. I want to go to bed with you. I'll pay.''

''How much?''

''A hundred dollars.''

One girl, bright, pretty, told me: ''It's like a fucking stock market or a department store. The prices vary according to what you get. French, that's say, eighty bucks. A straight lay can be anything — one hundred, two, or on a tough night and with an angry pimp, fifty dollars.''

We move on at the request of the police. The van rolls across Yonge onto Grosvenor Street. ''Boys' town,'' where young boys, ''chickens,'' try to turn tricks with gay men. Depending on what the john wants — blow job, holding hands — the rate is forty dollars and up. The kids are standing along the track in thin jeans, lightweight coats or windbreakers. It's cold out. As soon as the van pulls up they get in, shivering, their hands trembling from a combination of drugs and cold. I recognize one of them, Leo. He's been on television, in a program on street kids. But then it was summer and Leo was warm. Tonight he's cold. He hasn't turned a trick and he needs money.

Most of these kids have run away from home. Scott, a sixteen-year-old with long blond hair and the sort of looks that appeal to older men cruising the strip, sums it up: "I've had my fair share of home." In the corner John listens. He's a good-looking kid of seventeen or eighteen, but he seems older. His face is cut. He's wearing a red-checked winter coat, and as he takes a sandwich his hands tremble. He left home because he wasn't getting along with his parents: "Too many rules, they wanted to own you." And John didn't want to be owned. A constant theme emerges: freedom to do your own thing, becoming fed up with the rules. That's one side. There are also reasons such as sexual or physical abuse. Some kids leave home in search of the bright lights. Freedom. They come from small towns and cities, Saskatoon, Sudbury, or larger ones like Ottawa and Hamilton, from families where gay kids were not appreciated or wanted. One way or another they've been through the system — the children's aid, foster parents, group homes, correctional institutions. But tonight that's not the topic of conversation. Tonight they talk about their work, cops, johns, the weather, how to tell the bad guys. "Don't touch blacks, they'll rip you off, they're looking for a free ride." That's Zek, a worldly streetwise kid concealed behind a face that a choirmaster would love. He's got $5.45 in his pocket and he's got to get to Hamilton tonight. He's wearing a sports jacket over a thin sweatshirt. He carefully explains to me how to sort out good johns from bad. "Look at the eyes. If he blinks or seems hesitant, watch out. If you're in the car and he keeps looking at his rearview mirror, or doesn't look at you when you talk to him, get out."

"How do you learn all this?"

Leo cuts in, "You learn after you get ripped off a few times, then you learn." For some reason this triggers a heated debate, whether a straight can work the track. "No way," says Leo, "You have to be bisexual. You may do it once or twice as a straight but that's all, man, that's all." Zek argues that he's straight and Scott's straight and they are working. The debate goes on until the subject dies of its own accord, unresolved. Outside the cars cruise, men looking for boys. These are potential customers, sometimes called "suitor clones" because so many of them are businessmen or government employees. Someone says, "He's got one, he's okay, there he goes." *He* is one of the male hookers, and he's just entered a car. Negotiations are fast. Tonight these kids need the money.

The talk shifts back to the johns. The kids assure me that not all tricks turn out bad; in fact, "There are a lot of cool johns out there. . . . One invited me to stay with him over Christmas," John says. "No strings attached. And on Christmas Day he hands me this envelope, and I look inside and it's three hundred dollars." The other kids nod approval. But money doesn't come easy out here. To survive, they learn to "jack up," or rip off people or property, and they can show you how to make calls from a pay phone without using a quarter. Most of these kids have done time, for theft or breaking and entering, or have been taken in for soliciting or for indecent exposure. "There I was, man, and I'm in this car, and the guy asks me how much, and I say a hundred bucks. . . .'' That brings a chorus of, ''Never tell the price.'' ''Anyway,'' the story goes on, ''I tell him. And he says, did I tell you my name, and I say yes, it's Mike, and he says, no, it's Officer Mike. . . .'' They all laugh. Everyone has been bagged at some time, or almost. They tell stories of running through Queen's Park pursued by cops, or of being in cars where the drivers have panicked and ended up running into lamp poles.

These kids don't look different from most — except their eyes. Their eyes have lost their innocence. And behind the banter there is pathos: they fight over the hot-air vent from a building to keep warm, or get dumped out of a car in Brampton and have to get back to Toronto on a cold, black, winter night.

On another night, just behind the glitz of the Yonge Street strip, a few blocks north of the trappings of power and money, the towers of the city's financial center, another form of commerce is going on. It's at the street corners. Girls of all ages are selling them- selves. As the night wears on and as the bars close and the traffic increases, men, their inhibitions loosened by a few beers, cruise the track; some stop to negoti- ate a deal. The night is mild, the pavements wet from melting snow. The girls are tired. Two o'clock turns into three and the traffic eases, ''like shopping carts in a huge supermarket,'' one kid remarks. ''They're all looking to pick something off the shelf while com- parison shopping.'' She giggles at her remark.

The girls move to the doughnut shop. It's a neutral meeting ground, where hookers, street kids and assorted night people — jazz musicians off a gig, drunk native Canadians, pimps, taxi drivers, tow-truck drivers — share tables and stools. Three young men go into the back. Someone remarks that they're doing a deal. A jukebox plays a tune that no one is listening to. Two young men are sparring, throwing punches that don't land. One is thin with mop of hair and a wide smile, the other heavier, paunchy; he looks harder and older.

The girl behind the counter is tired and bored. She looks over and sees a group of Indians drinking out of large paper mugs. The counter girl is bored no longer. She goes over, seizes at the paper mug and tells the group, "You can't drink in this place. Get out, now!" She pries another mug loose from a hand and throws it in the garbage. The drinkers stagger out into the dark.

Drowsy pimps in high-fashion leather jackets sit with their backs resting against the counter. They're waiting for their girls to come in. The phone is in constant use. (Who do you call at three in the morning?) An attractive blond girl comes in and talks to a black pimp. She's saying that the cops have been cruising, putting a bit of heat on, but it hasn't been a bad night. Outside another couple is talking softly. He's her lover and pimp. A man in a blue Roots sweatshirt moves around, stoned. A group of Native Canadians come in, smashed on booze. This is where they will spend the rest of the night.

More girls come in. A jazz musician tells me to look at their boots. "See how wet they are? They been out there a long time standing on the corner waiting for customers." Most look like the kids you see hanging around suburban shopping malls. But they aren't your ordinary kids. They might have been at one time, but not now. Now they're working the streets, trying to survive.

One of them is Juanita, a pert kid, now seventeen. At age twelve she left Hamilton with her mother to live in Windsor. Mom was all right, except she had a few boyfriends, and one tried to rape Juanita. In the end he succeeded. So she left home and went to live with a succession of family friends. She dropped out of grade nine. She had no skills, a messy past and little future. So what does a kid like that do? She gets on a bus with a few bucks and heads for Toronto. She hustled here and there, did a few tricks, got tight with some friends and started doing drugs. But before she could work, she had to have a pimp to protect her turf from the other hookers and the other pimps. Meeting him wasn't hard.

What happened to her has happened and is happening to girls every day. "She gets off that bus at the Dundas station, and there's a pimp just waiting. And he knows just what kid is ripe for the taking. The signs: a single bag, a nervous look, an uncertain glance. They know how to play these kids, to press every button."

I'm talking to Constable Martin Zakrajsek, better known as Zak. He's a member of the Metro Toronto Police Juvenile Task Force. These are the cops who work downtown trying to get the under-sixteen-year-old hookers off the streets. "The pimps know more about the psychology of these kids than we ever will," Zak says. "They know the words, they tell these kids they're beautiful. In the slang of the street, the girl is being 'chumped off,' sweet-talked to get her to work for him. It's probably the first time the girl has heard anyone say she's pretty in her life. The pimps offer to buy them a meal, take them home, offer a bed, a place to stay. Once at the so-called home, the girl meets the pimp's 'wife.' That's a hooker who is living with the pimp. Usually the pimp will seduce the girl. Then, once she thinks she's in love with this guy, the 'wife' coaches the girl and they both start to nudge her onto the street. They talk about the easy money. The line is, 'After all, it's only sex, it won't hurt, we'll make sure you're taken care of.' And before you know it, there she is, on the track, with the pimp taking most of her money, and beating the hell out of her if she doesn't produce.''

Juanita lasted seven months in Toronto before going back to her mother in Windsor. But there wasn't the excitement of Toronto, so she left again. This time she went to Detroit, where she met Henry and moved in with him. Soon after she was back in Toronto to tell Leighton, her pimp, that she was carrying his child. Pregnancy hasn't kept her off the streets. She's still turning tricks while she supports a new boyfriend.

Near the doughnut shop is a hostel for transient kids. I sit at a table with two teenage girls, residents of the hostel. Outside the room, some kids are getting ready to bunk down on the floor. There are never enough beds to go around. A few are lucky enough to have a couch; most are already asleep in the hall. (The one thing street kids never get enough of is sleep.) The two girls have told me their real and their street names.

They are a study in contrasts, these two. One is tall, overweight, with dark blond hair. The other is small, almost petite, with huge dark eyes and dark hair cut straight. She is pregnant. Both are chain smokers. What they have in common is that they were street kids who survived and are trying hard to begin a new life. Their street names are "Mouse" and "Smurf," and that's the names I got to know them by.

For Mouse the first step toward doing tricks on a street corner began with rebellion against family rules. "My parents were warm, loving people," she says, "but they were too strict. My older sister experienced all the phases of growing up, but my mom wanted to protect me from the world." By age sixteen Mouse left home. Parents and child could not coexist. "I can't stand being in the same room with my parents. I can call on the phone, but no way in the same room." There were other rooms in Mouse's short life: jail cells, for example. That was because of a dangerous weapons charge. She had teamed up with a boy who got her on drugs, and her seventeenth birthday was spent in jail. From there it was a halfway house in Brampton.

"I can't really remember what happened. I was flipped out, standing on a street corner, in clothes that didn't belong to me. So I went home, and the next thing I knew I was having the shit beat out of me by four black guys, who tell me exactly what I'm supposed to do." What she was supposed to do was turn tricks. Her street companion was fifteen years old. Neither of them saw the hundreds of dollars they were making. The child she had was put up for adoption. "You can't get any lower than selling yourself on a street corner. We shouldn't be sold, shouldn't be used." But Mouse was. She was kept in line by beatings. Her days and nights were shrouded in pain and fear, fear for her life and the lives of her friends.

She tells of young girls who got out of line and ended up in the United States, dead, of others sold from pimp to pimp. "The johns were old, fat, desperate. And I was young, but God, you learn fast. Once I did a double trick, and the two of us got dumped out of the car in Mississauga with no money. We had to walk back to Toronto, and it was winter. When we got back, Pony, our pimp, just beat the hell out of us.'' She pauses. ''You know, being a woman sucks sometimes. We're the ones who are put out to work; we're the ones who take the beatings; it's the men who can take your cash and take your body.''

The only thing that got Mouse off the streets and got her away from the pimps who threatened her life was her boyfriend, who gave her what she had longed for — love without pain. It's his child she's carrying. He was the first man who didn't beat her up, a fact that still surprises Mouse, who came to believe that ''getting beat was the way it was.'' One boyfriend had cracked her ribs; another threw her out in the snow with her six-month-old child at four in the morning. ''I kept going back, because where else could I go? No one cared, and if you rat you could end up dead.'' Her anger and frustration build as she talks, and she starts to cry, quietly, hiding behind a cigarette, turning away.

Her friend doesn't cry. Smurf is older, harder, and she left no loving family behind. She is more typical of street kids. She was abandoned for four years by her mother; then her mother took her back. The mother had a succession of boyfriends, one of whom married the mother and raped Smurf when she was thirteen. She reported the attack by her stepfather, and was thrown out of the house. Her mother protected the husband by telling the police that her daughter was a chronic liar. In those days the police were not that sensitive to things like sexual abuse or domestic violence. It's no wonder there is a growing army of kids trying to escape.

"We are likely to see more family violence," says Brenda Rau, who works on the Hospital for Sick Children's child abuse team. "It's not just child abuse or wife battering. It's the whole issue of family violence. With wife battering, the children end up being emotionally abused. The whole issue of violence has to be looked at." A series of studies in Canada and the United States attempted to profile homeless kids who used shelters in major urban centres, such as Toronto and New York.[1] There have also been surveys of juvenile prostitutes in various Canadian cities.[2] It can be argued that the findings of these studies do not adequately reflect the population of homeless children, because less than half of homeless kids use shelters. But what emerges is a picture of grim despair, violence and deep psychological wounds. Thirty-six percent of the kids were fleeing sexual or physical abuse; forty-four percent were running from other long-term crises, such as drug abuse, alcoholic parents or step-family conflict; and twenty percent left because of problems arising from school, divorce or death. The executive director of the National Network of Runaway and Youth Services in the United States, June Bucy, puts the abuse figure as high as seventy percent.[3] That figure could be low. A recent Covenant House survey, which looked at all homeless kids and not just those working the streets, puts the incidence of some form of physical abuse at an alarming figure of eighty-six percent.[4]

The harsher forms of violence are perpetrated on females. Girls are punched, slapped, intentionally burned, hit with a belt or kicked. One out of every two males in the survey and eighty-six percent of the females had suffered an abusive sexual experience. For a third of the children, that experience was severe. The Committee on Sexual Offences against Children and Youths found that most girls working the street came from middle-class homes with a formal religious atmosphere, and that twenty percent had been subjected to a serious sexual assault as children. The figure for boys was ten percent.

The children's respectable middle-class homes were caldrons of tension, spousal anger, violence and alcoholism. The kids ran to escape. A group called National Youth in Care did a survey of juvenile prostitutes, male and female, and found that at least thirty-three percent had been abused, most of them sexually.[5] Another study found that almost all juvenile hookers were victims of multiple abuse in the home.[6] Half the females who are involved in prostitution have been victims of sexual abuse. A more recent survey involving six hundred street kids in Calgary found that half the kids left home because of "poor communications with their parents." One-third had been abused, and most of the females had suffered sexual abuse. Twenty percent fled because of drug- or alcohol-related problems within the family.[7]

There is another type of street kid, one that's often overlooked, the Native kid. "It's one of the most unaddressed problems in Canada," says John Turvey, a community youth worker in Vancouver's east end. "We're dealing with second and third generation street kids who are out on the street because their parents are out here, as well. They're molded to the life, they're sixteen or seventeen and they don't know damn all about school, but man, can they work the street. They pimp, they know how to do dope. These kids are so tough they laugh at pimps. Uptown where the white

kids are you get pimps. Down here the girls are working for the old man, and he'll kill any pimp who tries
to hustle in.'' Most have never had a full week with
their parents in their lives, and unlike middle-class
white kids they haven't any room to make moral
choices. These kids don't have a lot of choices to make
except how to survive. Their plight is made worse
when it comes to Native people, by the latent and rampant racism they face. There may be hostels and
shelters for runners, but the hostels are not in areas
where these kids live.

In other western cities, many of the Native street kids
are drifters. Some have family in the city, where they
crash, or they go back to the reserve, only to return
to the city streets. ''We're not looking at kids as
individuals, and certainly not Native kids,'' says Gary
Lack, one-time NDP MLA in British Columbia, who now
practices law. ''We are not reaching them; we haven't
the resources to do it.'' In Alberta, a judge remarks,
''We are not doing anything for Native kids. They are
probably dying. . . . They sure were before.''

No matter who they are or where they come from,
these kids share the problems that come from living
on the streets. Many suffer from psychiatric problems,
depression and suicidal tendencies; they lack life and
job skills. According to Toronto police staff sergeant
Les Douglas of the Youth Bureau, forty-four percent
of runaways under sixteen have been under some form
of institutional care: foster homes, group homes, detention centers. A third have had contact with child welfare. Many are functionally illiterate. That reality was
driven home to me when I was sitting with four street
kids in a restaurant on Dundas Street. I had met these
kids through Beat the Streets, a literacy program. I

asked them to read the menu. The kids took it up gingerly. "Can't do it." My first reaction was, this is Toronto, Canada; this isn't some third-world poverty-stricken nation. Why the hell can't these kids read? Why not? They couldn't read because they had quit school, quit their homes and worked the streets. These were the school castoffs, the ones the teachers ignored or worked out of the system, and here they were, trying to read a menu and not being able to.

Perhaps that's a minor problem when other problems are considered — the health problems these kids face, for example. Dr. Clyde Cave, a pediatrician at Toronto's Hospital for Sick Children, noted: "Street life severely affects physical health. Gonorrhea, chlamydia and urinary-tract and viral infections are common." He says that half the teen hookers he sees carry some type of sexually transmitted disease. More worrying is that these teenage hookers could be AIDS virus carriers. They may know everything about sex, be streetwise, use their bodies as the currency to buy drugs, food or affection, but they are often unaware of the latent dangers of random sex (though some have become so adept at using their mouth to put a rubber on a man that he doesn't ever know). AIDS is for someone else, not for them. If you add mainlining or shooting drugs to the sex, you can see the potential, ten years from now, for these kids and their bedmates to die very painfully.

These kids have made a decision. We might not agree with it or with how it's accomplished. Often the cure — running — ends up worse than the disease they ran from — home. The kids will say, however, that the violence, even the threats with weapons on the street, are less than what they had to face at home. But these kids, especially the young hookers, lived in an emotional void. Behind the tough facade — and sometimes the toughness went down to the core — was the comment, ''Maybe I will find someone who will care. Someone to love me.'' A large number would like to get off the streets. ''But where would I go? asks one hooker. ''I'm scared. My pimp would beat me, blow me away. . . . I need someone to talk to and to trust, who won't leave me. I need someone who cares.'' These kids were old enough or tough enough to make the choice, to pack and leave what to them was an untenable situation. What about the others, the kids who are too young, too scared, or don't see running as a way out? How many of them are there who are crying softly, but not being heard?

TWO

The Rights of Children

Almost ten years ago, I discovered that the Criminal Code of Canada allows for the use of force against children, within reason, of course. I thought that with all the concern for child abuse in the intervening years, the Code might have been changed. I called a family court judge and asked him to check on the status of Section 43 of the Criminal Code. "Yes, it's still here, and my book is right up to date."

> Every schoolteacher, parent or person standing in the place of a parent is justified in using force by way of correction toward a pupil or child, as the case may be, who is under his care, if the force does not exceed what is reasonable under the circumstances.

The learned judge was surprised that Section 43 still existed. Section 43 has been interpreted, on occasion, to exonerate parents who have abused their children. "Parents do have the right and indeed the obligation to impose discipline and punishment and the courts will not lightly interfere with this right. . . This right is recognized by our law in S. 43 of the Criminal Code of Canada."[1]

Just what rights do children have? From earliest

times, the reformers' desire to protect children and women within the home has run aground on the shoals of the so-called "family ideal": the firm belief that the family is private and should not be interfered with by the state. The family ideal accepts the fundamental principle that the father is the head of the household, that he has the right to his wife's body, and can punish her and the children. Under these rules, which still operate today, the family must be preserved whatever the cost to the individuals within it.

It is not surprising, therefore, to find that the evolution of children's rights has not been swift. History has it that around 2000 BC the king of Babylonia, Hammurabi, had put onto stone the known codified laws. There were thirty sections that dealt with the parent-child relationship. The thrust was to reinforce respect within the family. Parent-child reciprocal duties were defined, and were to exist as long as the child remained respectful and obedient. If the child disobeyed, the father could exact any form of punishment. Personal property, in this case a child, was more important than human life. An ancient Hebrew code, dating back to 800 BC, held infanticide as an acceptable practice. The Ten Commandments, which tell us to honor our mother and father, are silent when it comes to the obligation of parents to care for their children. Though the Talmud sanctifies the family and gives great emphasis to education, rabbis in the Middle Ages advised people that "to refrain from punishing a child will cause the child to become utterly depraved."[2]

In fact, whatever epoch one examines — Roman, Greek, Persian, Egyptian or Gallic — the father had absolute power over his children, even to the meting out of capital punishment. Anne Russell writes:

> According to Justinian, the Romans went fur-
> ther than any other legal system in placing the
> liberty and lives of children within the power
> of the father. These ancient Romans gave the
> father the power of life and death over his chil-
> dren upon the principle that he gave life and
> also had the power to take it away.[3]

This legal concept was known as *patria potestas*, and
under it the father could do anything with his children.
He could place them out for adoption, give them away
in marriage, carry out a divorce on their behalf, eman-
cipate them or put them to death. As Dr. Rafael Sajan
of Uruguay observed:

> Classical civil law set family relations on an
> authoritarian footing, conferring rights and
> powers on the head of the family in order that
> he may insure the union of the family group,
> and this did not allow for considerations such
> as the ''interest of the child.''[4]

The beginnings of English medieval law followed
Roman law with respect to children. However, the pas-
sage of time and economic necessity caused the old
order to soften. When children were put to work, they
attained economic importance and, with it, increased
status. And as the legal system expanded within
medieval England, so did the concept of *parens patriae*.
The Crown had the power and obligation to exercise
guardianship over persons who were incompetent,
mentally and physically, as well as over minors. It laid
the groundwork, which was to be refined at a much
later date, for the courts and the state to intervene to

protect children. This was not to be construed as a great leap forward in the application of humanitarian principles with respect to children. The concept had more to do with the disposition of wealth, property, land holdings and succession, where who got what meant who got power. While the father could still determine who received the inheritance and custody on the event of his death, the concept of *parens patriae* did place some limitation on his absolute power, and allowed the Crown to intervene on behalf of those who were unable to speak for themselves, including children of the poor and those who owned no property at all. But the concept was mainly used to protect the offspring of the rich and powerful, those the Crown felt had political and economic significance.

Another element had great significance in terms of child welfare and domestic violence: the status of women. Under canon law, which was based on the premise that man was created in the image of God, and under civil law, wife beating was acceptable practice, and the subjugation of women was taken for granted. By the thirteenth century, the only limitation placed on the husband's opportunity to use physical violence to discipline his wife was that he must have

The state of childhood as a unique period in a person's life, when the child is entitled to special care and consideration, is a relatively new concept, developed only in the last hundred years or so. In years past, parents were deemed to be free of their obligations once children could feed and clothe themselves. At five or six, children were expected to become members of the adult community, and by age seven, the child had attained the age of reason. But children were still being dumped into the streets like garbage. In 1780, about eight thousand children were abandoned in Paris and transported to poorhouses in boxes. Often a third of the children died in the boxes.[6] In England, the great jurist William Blackstone expounded the duties of the parents toward the child. These were maintenance, education and protection. But children were still regarded as chattels of the family or wards of the state, with no power and few legal rights.

As a new era of capitalism began in England in the late 1500s, the state began to intervene in the economy. Every boy had to serve a seven-year apprenticeship. But the apprenticeship program created poverty on a massive scale. To resolve the poverty and to help maintain social order, the Elizabethan Poor Relief Laws were implemented in 1601. These laws acknowledged that the state had an obligation to keep its people from starving. Other laws dealt with custody, claims of mothers and, in 1652, the establishment of workhouses. The most important feature of the Poor Laws is that they established, for the first time, a statutory duty that did not exist in the common law: family support. The children, parents and grandparents of a poor person had to support the poor person.

It was not until the industrial revolution that the state began to govern the treatment of children. The brutality of child labor in the "dark satanic mills" of England tweaked the moral conscience of the Victorians. Children were working fourteen hours a day in unimaginably bleak conditions: many died. Thousands of orphans had been bound over to factory owners by local parishes, who were trying to avoid paying maintenance costs for the children. Some children, to avoid the harshness of the mills, killed themselves. The government was forced to intervene, and in 1802, the first Factory Act was passed; it limited the hours a child could work each day. Conditions in Canada were not much better. Children could be bound over for an apprenticeship before the age of fourteen, a practice that lasted almost a hundred years.

The plight of children in the work force was alleviated as their economic importance declined, mainly because of improved technology. More important was the rise of labor unions. The unions fought long and hard to get children out of the factories for humanitarian reasons, as well as to create more jobs for adults.[7] It took time. In 1888, after the usual five-year commission of inquiry, the first Factory Act was passed in Canada. It removed some of the worst excesses of child labor. Girls younger than fourteen and boys younger than twelve were excluded from the work force and forbidden to operate machinery. Under the Regulation of Shops Act, children could work no more than seventy-four hours a week. As well, the first attempts were made at mass education. What all these acts translated into was not necessarily good for the child, who was becoming more dependent on the parents and state for longer periods of time. As the state took an interest in child welfare, rules and regulations were designed to govern the child's behavior. Truancy was punishable, and children were expected to behave in a socially acceptable manner. (Thus we have Section 43 of the Criminal Code, which absolved teachers, guardians and parents from being charged if they used force against a child, provided that force was reasonable.)

In the nineteenth century, the child-protection movement began to enjoy some success. The period produced the first hints of the concept of children's rights, which emerged as a logical extension of the British interest in animal rights. Animals were considered a mirror of Nature's designs. It was a short philosophical hop from animals to children.

The Royal Society for the Prevention of Cruelty to Animals was founded in 1824 in England; the American version was founded in 1866. The American Society for the Prevention of Cruelty to Animals (ASPCA) inadvertently became a means to protect children. In 1874 a church worker, making her rounds of a New York tenement, discovered a child who was being beaten by her parents and was suffering from neglect and malnutrition. The child was Mary Ellen Case; she was apparently the illegitimate daughter of one Mr. Francis Case. Francis had acquired a second wife, Mary Connolly, and it was observed that Mary Connolly "often beat the child, and sent her out in harsh weather with scanty bits of clothing." Appeals for action to the district attorney and the police were fruitless; the authorities did not wish to intervene in the family's affairs. Besides, a child was considered the parents' property.

Finally, in desperation, the young church worker appealed to Henry Bergh, the founder of the ASPCA. She argued that the child was a member of the animal kingdom and therefore must be protected. On that basis, the ASPCA brought action, which resulted in the child being removed from her family. One year later, five years after the founding of the ASPCA, the New York Society for the Prevention of Cruelty to Children was established.

Between 1874 and 1900, five hundred such societies were set up in the United States. The societies' mandate came from laws against abuse and neglect. Its agents' mandate came from the reasoning that, by rescuing children, they were saving them from a life of crime. Most of the agents spent their time pushing drunken, neglectful parents to take better care of their children. The society saw its role as preserving the family; it seldom removed a child. But at least children were getting some protection.[8] The old system of taking care of children in almshouses and orphan asylums or through indentured apprenticeships was changing. During the nineteenth century, an extensive system of foster care grew, as did child-saving efforts and institutions for children. By 1912, the Congress of the United States had passed child labor laws and had established a Children's Bureau, which had a mandate to report and investigate on matters ranging from orphanages to infant mortality.

In Britain, in a more oblique way, the right of the state to intervene on the behalf of the child was reinforced by the Liberal government. In 1906, the state provided free meals for impoverished schoolchildren. It was the first time the state stepped into what had been seen as a purely family function. In Canada, Toronto was the first city to provide for the maintenance of its children. The Province of Ontario was first to pass a Child Protection Act. It provided for the constitution of children's aid societies (CAS), and it gave the courts the power to commit neglected or delinquent children to the care of a children's aid society.

The Child Protection Act acknowledged that children needed protection from their parents. There is, however, a great gap between what protection is needed and what protection is provided. There have been some notable legislative measures to protect children, but the emphasis is still on preserving the family, not on the rights of children. While society has accepted that a child has a right to be adequately fed, clothed, housed and emotionally nurtured, there are no guidelines as to what is "adequate." Certainly the child doesn't have any say, nor can he or she ask for anything. Children are still seen as chattels, possessions of their parents. Parents still exercise the primary responsibility for the child, but the child's dependency has started to shift onto the shoulders of the state. One federal program, the Canada Assistance Plan of 1966 and 1967, is a landmark piece of legislation that provides federal funds for provincial services. These include a fifty-percent cost sharing for basic income services, including payments for kids in institutional care and foster homes. Government programs include a range of services, such as day care, medical care, family allowances, mothers' allowances and education. While the state is assuming a larger role in the life of the child by delivering these services, it is not asking the recipients if the programs are meeting their needs.

In *Beyond the Best Interests of the Child,* Joseph Goldstein, Anna Freud and Albert Solnit note that the child is singled out by law, as by custom, for special attention, and is distinguished from adults in physical, psychological and social terms.[9] Adults are recognized by law as being responsible for themselves and able to make their own decisions, in their own interests, free from government intrusion. It is a state of affairs that the authors, who are all eminently qualified — Goldstein is a lawyer and psychoanalyst, Freud a psychoanalyst and Solnit a pediatrician and psychiatrist — fully support. They start with the premise that only after the family fails in its function should the child's interests become a matter for state intrusion. This premise is the basis of child protection and child rights. The Ontario Law Reform Commission emphasized that there must be the probability of ''permanent harm'' before the state has the right to intervene. The Commission noted the traditional rights of the family in our culture, and then stated:

> We align ourselves firmly with those whose opinion it is that the power of the state to intervene in the relationship between parent and child should be used only when there is reasonable justification for the belief that a child will be harmed permanently by the conduct of its parents.[10]

Children, on the other hand, are not regarded as being competent to determine or safeguard their own interests. They are dependent and in need of continuous care by adults, who are committed to take on the responsibility. Parents have obligations toward their children under the law, but the children have no rights to demand anything from the parents. They must rely on the good faith of adults, and on the law. If the adults fail, then the law will intervene, not because the children have rights, but because the parents have failed.

In 1975, a report called *Child Abuse and Neglect* was sent to the House of Commons Standing Committee on Health, Welfare and Social Affairs. The report pointed out that:

> Among the issues involved in providing preventive services to children and families, the question kept arising ''what are the rights of the child?'' and ''what are the rights of the par-

ents?'' It was made clear by a number of witnesses that by tradition and law the rights of
the parent have always superseded those of the
child unless and until the breakdown of the
family necessitated the intervention of a public authority.[11]

Our society places the rights of the family above the
rights of the individuals within it; we emphasize the
obligations of the parents rather than the rights of the
child. These social attitudes create tensions that are not
easily resolved.[12] The children's advocate of British
Columbia, Allison Burnett, said, ''Children's rights are
very difficult for adults to deal with. They cannot get
their minds around the idea that a child might
challenge their judgments or decisions.''

In the United States, children might challenge adults
through the courts. The California Supreme Court has
held that a battered child who was returned to his
family and suffered further harm can sue the authorities who discharged him into the family's care. The
courts have also applied the fourteenth amendment,
which concerns due process, to children contesting
their committal by parents to mental institutions. And
the United States Supreme Court has upheld the right
of a teenager to secure an abortion without gaining
parental consent.

In Canada, the Charter of Rights has yet to affect children. Recently, the Supreme Court of the Province of
British Columbia dealt with a case that involved the
parents of a six-year-old with severe brain damage.
Doctors suggested a brain operation. The parents
wanted to postpone the operation, preferring that the
child die rather than be subjected to more pain with

no guarantee as to the outcome. The prognosis was that if the child did not die, he could well end up living a life of increasing distress. The court held that, regardless of his condition, the child had the right to live. The decision implied that the child had rights beyond the jurisdiction of the parents. Although the judgment did not specifically refer to children's rights, it assumed that a severely handicapped child has the same basic rights as other individuals in Canada.[13]

Society must insure that the needs of children are met while their rights are acknowledged. We must also find a balance between the adults' authority and accountability. Nowhere does the conflict emerge more dramatically than within the child welfare system. This system begins in the family court.

THREE

That's the Law

"We are talking power. What people see in child welfare agencies, whether it's human resources in British Columbia or social services in Newfoundland or the children's aid in Ontario, is the power to remove the child, to wrench the family apart. Not even the police have that power." So summed up one judge. That power is often an infringement of the basic rights of the parents, the family and the child in pursuit of some solution to a child's problem. There is an assumption that, in the last resort, the state, through its agencies, is the final arbiter of how parents can raise their children.

But the state's power is tempered by the reality that the rights of the parents are still viewed as paramount, in most instances, by the courts, and certainly by legislation, and that parents can sometimes compromise the best interests of the child. Mary McCovell, of Toronto's Covenant House, explained: "The problem is that while the professionals can give you a definition of what adequate parenting should be, it would be torn to shreds by the legal community. It happens every day in court, where no one is prepared to lay out what is proper parenting."

In the end, the courts must provide the definitions and the rules, and decide what is in the best interests of the child. Says Peter Fraser, chairman of the British

Columbia Lawyers Apprehension Committee: ''The judge is in a position of playing God, but he or she is dependent on other people's information in a highly charged and emotional situation. It's one of the toughest jobs in the legal profession.''

Child welfare is usually the responsibility of the provinces, with the federal government involved only as a provider of cash for various programs. The provinces, directly or indirectly, run the child-protection services and pass the laws that say when and how the authorities or agencies can intervene to protect a child. Cases involving child protection are fought out within the provincial family courts. The biggest family court in Canada is in Toronto, on Jarvis Street.

The building is squat, ugly and forbidding. It looks far more like a machine-gun emplacement than Canada's busiest family court. It does more custody cases and more child protection cases than any other court in Canada. One judge said sadly, ''But look at it.'' Look, indeed. Inside, the corridors reek of neglect and public indifference. The public waiting area contains grimy, shoddy furniture. There is no hint that this is a place that deals with people, often frightened, angry people whose lives will be strung out for all to look at. Nowhere is there any relief: no plants, no magazines, no toys. There used to be a play area with a supervisor, but the province abandoned the idea because it was too costly. The corridors are crowded with lawyers trying to communicate with clients; there are no rooms for them to use. The air-conditioning has failed again.

The condition of the building has forced even the judges to get angry. ''We have demanded,'' one said,

"that the court be refurbished, to make it more present-
able, so people would be treated with more respect.
What we heard from the powers that be is that it is
not in our jurisdiction to give you new benches, but
we have some benches from the Ottawa courthouse
you can take. God almighty, the Ottawa courthouse
is as bad as this one!" Another judge added, "We do
not have any control over what shape our courtroom
is in, or even over our secretaries. But worse — take
a look. There is no place for lawyers to take their clients.
If I want a pretrial conference, I have to bring them
into my office or find a courtroom that might be empty.
That is one hell of a way to run a system." Toronto
writer June Callwood summed it up when she pointed
out the "disgraceful condition of Toronto's largest
family court . . . one indicator of the indifference to the
lives of these butchered children."

At least Toronto has a courthouse. In many small
towns the family court can be anywhere: a restaurant,
a schoolroom. Often lawyers and clients meet in the
lawyer's car. One judge, the Honorable T.G. Zuber,
wrote, "In some areas, the choice of a court location
threatens to bring the administration of justice into dis-
repute. Some courts are housed in shopping centers,
in hotels, beside taverns, or in one case, in a Lions Club
dance hall, right beside the bar, over which hung a
toilet seat."[1] There is a chronic lack of funding for the
courts, and the courts have little control over how the
money is spent. Trying to get a new typewriter is a
major fight; hiring new staff is almost impossible.

Yet with each passing year, more legislation is passed
dealing with the family. One senior judge, the Honorable Lucien Beaulieu, noted that, "We have the Family
Law Reform Act, the Child and Family Services, and

the Young Offenders Act; all have expanded the role of the courts. At the same time there has been little done to improve the quality of the system to take care of the quality of matters before it.'' Judge Zuber has written:

> It should be a general principle of government to assess the cost of implementing legislation which will affect the courts as part of the cost of the legislation itself. If the government cannot afford the cost of implementing the legislation, it cannot afford to pass the legislation.[2]

One problem is conveniently forgotten by the lawmakers, who are far removed from the family courts: the only judge ever murdered in a courtroom was a family court judge. Two lawyers have been killed in the past decade; one was involved in a terrorism case and the other was pleading a case in a family court.

Judges in family court have to be on their toes all the time. One explained, ''We have conferences about what to do if it starts to blow up. You cannot walk into this court in a bad mood and snap at someone, because they are so wound up they twang, and they are likely to snap and come right at you.'' Judge Beaulieu remarked, ''I have a constant worry about security, especially in a court that is dealing with highly emotional issues that cut at the very core of family relationships.''

As the representative of His Majesty, the judge sits, gowned, above the courtroom fray both physically and emotionally. Before him are the legal counsels. On the right is the witness stand. Behind the first table sit other interested parties — the social workers, the parents. Behind that row sits the public. The judges have years of legal training, practice before the bar and books of case histories and precedents that explain the well-trod pathways of legal jurisprudence. They listen, seek guidance if necessary from what has gone before, apply wisdom and understanding to the case at hand, with fairness and compassion, but always within the letter of the law.

The people who are enmeshed in child-abuse hearings generally are not affluent. To them, the family court is just another arm of the bureaucracy that has invaded their lives and exercised some form of control, like the police, the public health nurse, the probation officer, the truancy officer, the mother's allowance worker, the child-protection agencies. "The only conclusion one can come to," one social worker said, "is that we have a system that borders on the arbitrary to control the poor, and the courts are perceived as just another vehicle for that control." One judge noted: "When a mother, stressed, harassed by the profusion of officials, complains, demands that they get off her back, she is seen as being hostile, and the professionals who are dealing with that woman will make sure that attitude is put before the court." Judge Zuber reported that there is a profound class separation in the courts:

> In the 19th century English Magistrates had been given jurisdiction by a number of Acts designed to protect deserted wives and children. . . . The clientele of the English and Canadian magistrate was mostly the poor. Complaints involving deserted or assaulted

wives, truancy, and juvenile delinquency almost always were directed against members of lower income families.[3]

The family division of the provincial court is still largely for the poor. Some lawyers boast that they have never taken a case in family court; judges and lawyers complain that the family division does not rank with the higher courts. Large numbers of people who come to the family courts rely on legal aid; they cannot afford their own lawyers. One judge remarked, ''Lawyers come in ill prepared. Many are straight out of law school. They come, with middle-class backgrounds, from law schools that teach you how to read books but not how to prepare a case for hearing. And too many are just incompetent.'' Only now are some law schools beginning to teach students about the realities of family law: that it deals with people; that the courts are not there for the benefit of counsel, but to serve the public; and that the justice system deals with social issues.

Yet family court judges are making decisions that can affect the lives of families for years. Mistakes made in the family courts can cost society dearly. One judge said, ''There are times when I can see thirty years later the same person, this time a parent, standing before the court, accused of abusing his child, as he or she was abused as a child, and I ask if I have made the right decision.''

The decision-making starts when the child-protection or welfare worker decides that, under existing provincial legislation, a child is in need of protection. The worker must decide if the child has suffered, or if there is substantial risk that the child will suffer physical harm, sexual molestation or sexual exploitation, emotional harm (demonstrated by severe anxiety, depression, withdrawal) or self-destructive behavior. Child welfare agencies can intervene if a child needs treatment for a medical problem or suffers from a mental, emotional or developmental problem and the person in charge refuses to or is unable to provide that treatment.

The Young Offender Act also lists reasons a child up to the age of twelve can be apprehended by a child welfare agency, for example if the child causes bodily injury or property damage. The agency can intervene if a child has been abandoned. Children older than twelve can be brought before the court with their consent. Younger children need the consent of the parents. The consent cases are increasing as parents, unable to cope emotionally or financially or unable to control the child, look to the state for help. Often the parent allows the agency to provide short-term care for the child. ''In a lot of cases, the short term becomes the long term, as parents simply walk away from the kid,'' one social worker noted. In Alberta, the care can extend for two years; then the child goes back to the family or is made a ward of the crown.

Intervention by the agency begins with a complaint. By law, all professionals who work with children must report suspicions of and actual cases of abuse. Most child-protection workers say that professionals, for example doctors, who were once loath to inform on their middle-class patients, are now more willing to come forward. Gary Lack, a British Columbia lawyer and a former NDP MLA, claims, ''Some doctors still do not report. Some are frightened of destroying the family, even though there were clear, unmistakable signs of abuse.''

Some provinces have twenty-four-hour abuse hot lines, where anyone can report child abuse. (Most child welfare agencies have such a service, but callers are more willing to use a service where they do not have to give their names.) Once a complaint is received, an investigation is carried out by a child-protection worker. Manuals lay down the procedures to be followed. "But in the end it comes down to common sense, experience and a lot of gut feeling," said Barbara, a worker who has twenty years' experience in the field. The decision to apprehend a child is not made lightly. The worker must ask these questions: How serious is the abuse? Is it an isolated incident? Can the parents alter their behavior or accept help? Does the family have a record of abuse? In any instance where the child seems to be in physical danger, the child-care worker or a police officer can forcefully remove the child without a warrant. In a situation where the family denies the worker access to the child, the worker can apply for a warrant to enter the home.

From then on, it's the protection worker against the parents, with the child in the middle. The worker starts to collect evidence to substantiate the removal of the child. The paper war begins. There are team meetings and discussions with the lawyer for the child welfare agency. The parents are told their rights, and the legal process is explained.

Within five days, the child-protection worker must appear before the court to state the reasons for apprehending the child. In some provinces, a lawyer is appointed for the child, to insure that the focus is on the child, not the agency or the parents. In other provinces, the agency speaks for the child. This system sometimes causes a conflict of interest, because the child welfare agency has its own turf to defend. What it wants may not be what the child needs. Another problem is the quality of legal counsel. Lawyers who deal with child welfare cases complain that lawyers for the other side are often ill prepared. Some don't spend enough time with their clients; others are not ready for court.

Financial constraints play a role. Only a few children's aid societies can afford to keep a lawyer on staff. In many cases, the Crown or the child-protection worker represents the agency, and supposedly the child. Legal representation for the child is uneven across Canada. Ontario now has lawyers who have taken courses on representing children. Professor Bernard Dickins of the University of Toronto's Faculty of Law says, "This is an indication that the courts recognize that quite young people need independent legal representation even if the child is not old enough to give instruction to the counsel." Ontario also has a new official guardian, Willson McTavish. Under McTavish, patronage went out and competence came in. In British Columbia, children receive the benefit of a full-time child advocate, who is on the staff of the attorney general.

The initial court hearing can be clean and quick, depending on the judge and the attitudes of the parents and the child. The key issue is often whether the parents will retain custody until the protection hearing, which can take up to a year to arrange. Sometimes all sides fight it out to decide where the child will end up. Another question is whether the parents will have access to the child during this period. Some lawyers say that access is used as a weapon, to whip the parents into line. One solution is for the child to be returned home under the supervision of a child-care worker or family worker. Then the agency must try to provide the staff to do the supervision.

It all comes back to money. Ontario has family support workers, who work with the parents and help the family deal with its problems. British Columbia has no similar program, partly because of the province's budget cuts. Instead, there are social workers with large caseloads. Newfoundland has a Child Abuse Treatment and Prevention Unit, which co-ordinates the response to child-abuse cases and refers families to available services.

After the first apprehension hearing, there is a protection hearing, where the final disposition of the child is decided. Before the protection hearing, there must be an assessment of the child. In large urban areas with good facilities, an assessment might be done in a few weeks. In other areas, an assessment might take months.

After the assessment is done, then it's back to court, sometimes with three lawyers involved. Representation for the child is at the court's discretion, but it is becoming common, except in British Columbia, where funding is being cut back, a trial will go on as long as necessary. But cases in family courts are fragmented. A hearing starts, gets postponed, gets underway again.

But it is not that simple. The case starts with the "discovery," held between the lawyers in a neutral office. There documents are exchanged, reports looked at, directives pondered. Lawyers can ask what this document means, what the information is all about. The lawyers can determine if there is any information lacking that they can ask the court to demand be presented. After discovery, both sides go to a pretrial (often misnamed a presettlement) conference, what judges call "informal meetings between the parties." The system is logical, which naturally, means that it is not universal, and not mandatory, and many judges refuse to use it. A judge I talked to explained, '' What happens is that when we see that a case is going to trial we demand a pretrial which is held before. Everything is confidential and off the record. You talk to the lawyers, tell them what you think about the case; you can let your hair down and say exactly how you think the case will go. Here is where you find out how prepared the lawyers are, have they been talking with their clients, and where I as a judge can find out what hasn't been told to the other side.''

It is also the moment when the judge can remind all concerned that it's the best interests of the child that the hearing is all about: not professionals' or the legal counsel's feelings. It is not uncommon for the lawyers to tell the judge in these meetings that ''my client is a bitch,'' or ''the father is a bastard.'' Thus forearmed, the Judge has a better idea of the personalities, and can help get the lawyer ''off the hook'' by allowing him or her to say to the client, ''I told you so.''

If a settlement cannot be worked out, then at least the issues where there is agreement can be worked out, and those in contention narrowed down, the direction of the trial laid out, the number of witnessess defined, and the time they need to be present determined. ''The whole thing helps to speed up the process, and of course if possible to avoid going to trial,'' Judge Beaulieu explained. Marilyn McCormack described the situation: ''Usually we have an arrangement whereby the lawyers will ask for a meeting with all the parties concerned, where they will discuss the case and see if anything can be worked out without going to trial.'' While lawyers are committed by their profession to defend and represent their clients to the best of their ability, ''when kids are involved as the third party most affected, often the lawyers will accept that winning for their client might mean losing for the child." One lawyer said. "It does not happen often, but it does." Peter Fraser put it as a conflict between loyalty to the client, in this case a parent, and a higher duty to the child. "So far I have been lucky. I have not had to make the choice, but it could come." "That is why," another lawyer explained, "I will never defend a parent who is acccused of sexual abuse. I could not do a proper job emotionally." Laywers who do practice in the family courts tell of the constant strain, and a feeling that "a lot of lawyers do not have the toughness to take the cases we do."

Most lawyers who have been involved prefer to have a pretrial conference. One of the recommendations of Fraser's British Columbia Lawyers Apprehension Committee is a mandatory meeting of all the parties concerned to see if a solution can be worked out regarding the child's future without having to go to a full-blown protection hearing. It can save days of litigation tying up the courts' time, with trials now lasting two to three weeks which before were a matter of days. Often a lawyer says that "I'm here because I have to be, but I know that my client will not be successful, but I can't bend him." On occasion the judge will inform the client of that reality. One judge, a veteran of the family court, complained, "It is often the judges who have to remind the parties that the issue is the future of the child, which is sometimes forgotten as each side gets into a "must-win" frame of mind." One lawyer angrily claimed that the children's aid can be "bloody vindictive. They do not like some low-income, unkempt parent, or some single mother challenging their wisdom." It is an observation that Judge Beaulieu agrees with, "On occasion, the CAS, or even other professionals, are affronted if you question their assessments."

Once the case does get a full protection hearing, the child-care worker presents the circumstances surrounding the apprehension of the child. The agency must produce a plan for the child. The child-care worker or intake worker might be the only one asked to testify; sometimes the parents are asked by the judge if there is anything they want to add. Unfortunately, the plans for the child might not be in the child's best interests. One child advocate explained that a plan might be based on incomplete information. This happens because child welfare agencies do not have unlimited funds for psychiatrists, psychologists, group homes or other facilities that might be required. "Kids are not important enough to warrant large expenditures of public money," one judge explained.

The hearings are "civil," which means that, at the proceedings, the parents or guardians will not be held criminally responsible for their behavior. It also means that the child welfare agency does not have to prove neglect or abuse beyond reasonable doubt. (In a criminal proceeding they do.) The agency or its lawyers must establish that the child needs to be protected. Often, judges will admit hearsay evidence, or will take circumstances into account. For example, a child might have suffered bruises or injuries that, in an expert's opinion, were not accidental, even though no one witnessed the child being beaten. The admitting of hearsay or circumstantial evidence is vital, as most abuse takes place within the privacy of the home, where the only witnesses are family members, the abused child and the abuser. Most children are too scared or too young to talk. (Children are often told that if they tell on Mommy she will be taken away to jail, and the children will be held responsible for breaking up the family. Or they are told that no one will talk to them again.) It takes a lot of courage for a young child to recount, in the intimidating atmosphere of a court, what went on at home. And even where judges try to make children comfortable — they have been known to hold children on their laps to ease the children's fears — it is a lot to ask of children that they turn against their parents.

Critics of the family court say that parents, children and child welfare agencies use the courts as diagnostic and therapeutic vehicles. They look to the judge to tell them what should happen to the child, where the child should be placed. Often it is not for want of ideas, but simply because they have run out of resources and hope. "We [the courts] are not here to be social workers," says Judge Beaulieu. "Our power is limited to what is laid down in the act. We can order an assessment and we can impose terms and conditions on the parents, the society or the child. But we cannot conjure up resources that are not there." "But at least," added another judge, "the professionals with experience have the courage to say, 'Hey, what do we do now? This is a problem we cannot handle. Then at least the problem is laid out in front of you. What angers me is the times when society screws around with all kinds of experiments, without reasoning it out or explaining why they are doing it."

The various child welfare acts in Canada are designed to keep the child at home, although the home might not always be the best environment. A child welfare agency must have a strong argument if it wants to remove a child from the home.

It might seem, from a quick examination of the legal procedures, that the child is well served, that the rights of the child are assured. But that is not the case. "The judicial system still has problems, as do most adults, with the concept of children's rights," explains Allison Burnett, British Columbia's child advocate. Courts can become prejudiced against parents because of signs of poverty; because the parents live on welfare; because a home is described as dirty. (The idea of a dirty home does not sit well with middle-class values.) But poverty is something that judges need to be sensitized to. As well, lawyers and social workers need to be sensitized to the needs of their clients.

In Ontario, some of the lawyers who represent children for the Official Guardians Office are inexperienced articling students. (Judges can remove an articling student if they feel the case has not been properly represented.) More worrisome is the lack of uniform representation for children in the courts.

Often what the child needs in court is not what the agency can provide. One lawyer, Lonny Mark, describes how he handles his cases. "When I represent a child, the child is the boss, and that's who I take my instructions from. I meet the child, sit down and tell who I am, find out if the child understands what is happening. I then ask how the CAS is doing. Are the parents allowed access? In most cases the kids want to go home or go to a group home. They also want to get the CAS out of their lives."

Representing children younger than five is not easy. There is a difference between the child who has been in school and one who hasn't. The child who's been to school for even six months is much better able to understand what is going on, and to communicate with adults. Another problem is that judges who work in the family court are not all competent. The judge must balance the interests of society against the best interests of the child and come to a conclusion that satisfies everyone. Unfortunately judges are human, and have the same prejudices as other members of society.

It is getting close to eleven in the morning. For more than two and a half hours, Judge Beaulieu has been talking about the family courts. His descriptions are clear. He knows the territory — he was a social worker before he went to law school. His secretary and other staff are indicating that the court demands his attention: there are cases, meetings, conferences. "Sometimes I ask what keeps me and my colleagues going. We are the ones who have to deal with four-year-old children who were sexually assaulted and had their vaginas ripped apart. We listen to evidence of children burned with cigarettes, smashed against walls, brutalized in communities of religious or satanic cults. We have to deal with perversions, torture, the belt buckle marks on a baby's back, the scars. . . ." Another judge commented, "I thought I knew about life, but what I have seen as a family court judge makes me feel sick. Bestiality, buggery. . . I have seen instances of kids lying in a crib for two weeks and the mother just sitting there. They take the child to the hospital, and they can't get the kid off the mattress because the child's skin has rotted right off."[4] Another judge commented, "I know some of my colleagues refuse to hear these cases. They are burned out, and they employ every device to avoid dealing with it." These judges have become frustrated with a system that does not provide the money or resources to deal with the problems of child welfare.

"We are not miracle workers," one judge explains. "We have to deal with what is available, and often it is not much. Sometimes I ask myself if the court system is the best way to resolve issues involving children. But it is the only system we have, so we have to make it work."

FOUR

The Other Side of the Hill

There are nearly seventy-five thousand children in care at any one time in Canada. These are kids that society, through its agencies, has decided are in need of protection. They are in care because the parent or parents have decided that keeping the child is too much strain, financially or emotionally. Some of these children have been thrown away by their family; others have run. A few have sought the protection of a child welfare agency after deciding that seeking intervention is better than living in the hell of the family home. They have come from homes that were, to use the lexicon of the child welfare agencies, "unsatisfactory." Most of these children have suffered physical, emotional or sexual abuse, as well as neglect. They have psychological scars that will be there for the rest of their lives. All these kids have one thing in common: a need to be wanted and loved.

These kids have been through the system, the same system that prompted one social worker to remark, "I don't know who the hell we are working for, the kids or the system. Sometimes I think it's the system."

These kids have been neglected, brutalized and assaulted, and are now being shunted through a series of often indifferent care givers. The kids will end up populating the jails and mental hospitals, will work on the streets, drop out of school, be unemployed. Yes, indeed, they are part of the system; they are the reason for it. The care of our children has evolved into a bureaucratic structure, an industry. Taking care of kids is the game, but the kids do not have much input about the rules by which the game is played. Experts, government agencies and private or public agencies make the rules. No one asks the kids.

Her name is Kim. She's an attractive seventeen-year-old, bright, with the wide-spaced eyes one associates with people from the vast prairie provinces. Her life was lived in a succession of cities and towns as her parents chased some dream that never seemed to materialize, and each town seemed to be a notch down the economic ladder. Kim is not a classic case of abuse. She was not subjected to physical violence, nor was she sexually molested. What Kim got was indifference. Her memories were of parents who saw her as an encumbrance, one they would dearly like to be rid of. When Kim was six, they did. She was put into the care of the children's aid society. "I could not believe that my parents did not want me," Kim says. "I felt it was my fault, that I hadn't tried hard enough. Here I was in this strange home with other kids, some who were like me, in care, and others who were the foster parents' kids. I felt we were second-class people, that the foster parents' natural kids came first. I cried a lot, and when I went to school and kids asked me where I lived, I would lie, because foster kids were looked down on." Kim did not last too long at her first "placement." The foster parents did not like Kim, and they thought she was rebellious. "My social worker used to come by once a month. She always acted as if I was bothering her, like taking up her time when she could be doing something else. I never believed she cared about me at all. I was just another file in her fucking caseload.''

Kim packed her belongings and moved to another foster home and another school. ''I still wanted to go home, and I still could not accept that my parents did not want me back. I wish the social workers had the guts to get my parents to tell me that to my face. But they never did. So I kept this hidden hope; I called it my hope for home. But it never happened.'' Instead, Kim found a measure of security and happiness. ''I loved my new foster parents. Sure, they weren't my real parents, but they gave me a sense of security, and they listened, and I really felt I was one of the family.'' It was not to last. The foster parents thought they were being abused by the children's aid. They thought they were a dumping ground for emotionally disturbed teenagers. And they wanted to travel. ''As my foster mom said, 'If we don't go now, we never will.' I think they came into some cash from her mom dying. They traveled, and so did I.''

Once again Kim packed her bags. It was becoming obvious to Kim that she had no control over where she was to live, no control over her life. ''The next foster parents were hell. They lived by a mass of rules and regulations. It was like a prison. The foster parents were in it for the money. All I was there for was to be their little maid. Their own kids ate better than I did, and I spent most of my time in my room, which I called a cell. I kept saying to myself, I'm Little Orphan Annie, only I'm not really an orphan. I have parents. I went to a new school and tried to make new friends. But I didn't trust any of the social workers. To me they were all fucking liars.''

Kim had few friends, and the effects of the shuffling from one foster home to another showed up in her schoolwork. Her grades did not reflect her ability, much to the annoyance of her teachers. Kim's social worker seemed to Kim ''so neat and tidy. Her life was fine. I would tell her things and she would tell the foster parents, so I wouldn't tell her anything anymore.'' A psychological assessment of Kim was done, but the results were never told to her. She assumes she didn't do well. ''I was pissed off, and hated the foster home, and I detested the social worker, who was just too nice to be true. That's when she wasn't blabbing to the foster parents. You know what she reminded me of? A fat hen, all prim and feathers, sitting on an egg. I saw her clucking about me to her friends in the children's aid barnyard.''

Faced with adult betrayal, and with no control over her existence, Kim started to rebel. In the words of the CAS, ''The placement was breaking down.'' And when the placement breaks down, you move the child. So Kim moved again, this time more than eighty kilometers, to a much smaller community. New foster parents, a new social worker. (Kim was moved out of town because of a desperate shortage of foster homes, especially for teenagers.) Kim felt unwanted, ''like a bag of garbage that was moving drom dump to dump.'' She felt that she was not accepted or loved. ''I wanted to be in my own home, though I knew that was never going to happen. You know how I found out? Not from the social workers, but from my mom, who told the judge in family court — 'No. I do not want her back.' That was one of the most miserable days of my life. Learning that your own mother doesn't want you.''

In her new home Kim felt isolated; she also felt out

of place in the local school. She had no friends, and in the small community she was ostracized because she lived in a foster home. Her social worker offered little support. "She was okay, I guess," Kim recalls, "but I think she was really hassled with other worries that might have been more serious. I don't know. I kept trying to tell her that I wanted out of the home, and all she would say is that she would see what she could do. She didn't." So Kim ran away. She was thirteen, tall for her age. She hitchhiked to Toronto and tried to find her parents. "Maybe they had changed their minds. That was my dream." But they had moved, and no one knew where they had gone.

"I guess that finally convinced me that I had no family. So there I was, a few bucks in my purse, a knapsack with some clothes, nowhere to stay, no friends, and shit scared. What do I do now? I found a doughnut shop and stayed there the first night. All the time I was hustled by these black guys. I didn't know what they were then. I do now. They were pimps. They wanted me to work for them. They kept telling me how beautiful I was, and how they would give me a place to stay and some money. I guess I was just too scared or too stupid. Anyway, I said no. All night long, until about three in the morning, these girls would come in with these really short minis or tight jeans. They would use the john, have a coffee and then go out again. I would see cars stop and they would talk to the drivers. Suddenly it clicked: they're prostitutes. God, was I naive."

During the night Kim met a couple of other street kids who had found a place to crash. She teamed up with them and ended up in an abandoned building slated for demolition. The street kids stayed alive by stealing and selling drugs. For Kim it was a new freedom, no rules. But the freedom didn't last. The police picked Kim up, and she was returned to the children's aid. But at least they got the message that Kim didn't like her foster home. The children's aid moved her back to the city. It was Kim's fifth placement, and it was one of the worst periods of her life. She felt she knew how to adjust to new foster parents, new rules, new expectations. She usually saw her social worker — her seventh — about once every two or three months. Kim was not regarded as a "special case" by her worker, who accorded Kim a low priority. By children's aid standards, the worker's assessment was right; the workers had far more pressing cases to cope with.

Kim thought her worker didn't listen to her. "She would say she understood. I don't know why the hell she was talking about understanding. She came from a nice home with a nice family. Her parents didn't put her into care. What did she know about how I was feeling?" It may have given Kim some satisfaction to know that a lot of foster-parent families felt the child welfare agencies did not listen to them, either. Like Kim, they felt they were on their own.

Kim would find out just how alone she was. She had some idea about her rights: she had been given a booklet outlining the nineteen rights of children in care, ranging from discipline to medical care to clothing. Not that the booklet meant much: rights are only rights when they can be enforced and when someone is present to see that they are enforced. (A lot of foster parents complain that foster kids have too many rights.) Kids in care are subjected to the foster parents, or to whatever institutional environment they find themselves in.

Kim's new placement was no loving family — it was "hard time," to use a prison expression. One of the foster kids in the home was a teenage male who had a history of aggression. He was there because the children's aid did not have a specialized placement for him. (The number of vacancies for kids who need special treatment and counseling has dropped as the demand has increased.) "There were four of us," Kim says. "Three were off the wall. One guy went around spraying fuck you on the walls. Another, when he got pissed off, would kick the walls in. The other girl had been abused by her parents and was in bad shape. She would cry and yell or become moody. She told me that she was reliving a nightmare all the time. She once said that no one would believe her when she told them what was happening. She was full of hate for her parents."

The tension, the violence, the fights between the two boys began to take their toll. Kim's school grades slid. She felt that every day she was returning to a battleground. The foster parents seemed unable or unwilling to control what was happening. Kim is a perceptive girl, and she realized something was wrong. "What was wrong was that the foster parents had given up. They seemed beaten. The case worker told me they just could not cope. I guess they were exhausted, like I was," said Kim. "I mean, who could take that day after day? I remember the wife calling the children's aid and asking for a worker to come over to help. But apparently no one was around. I think that was when they decided to stop being foster parents."

Kim went to her sixth placement. This time was was lucky. Child and foster parents matched. "I finally felt as if I was actually cared for, loved. I needed that so badly. They made me part of the family, and I remember when I began calling them mom and dad. I think that was when I realized that I had cut off my natural parents. I even got a social worker who listened. She became a friend. She never looked at her watch, she never told the foster parents things that I said were just between the two of us. We used to go out for lunch.''

Kim's odyssey through the system underlines the anger and helplessness many of these kids feel. They are caught up in a bureaucracy they do not understand and cannot control. They are in care because there is no alternative. They are in care because child welfare agencies failed to keep the family together. They are the product of abuse, of parental unwillingness or inability to care for them. These kids start with a lot of anger and emotional turmoil, and they feel betrayed and unloved. They have waited in receiving homes, often for months, while the CAS tries to get an assessment done. Then they are moved through the system. They will tell you that nobody wants them. They have a sense of being different. And they are different — they have been taken from their families, or have run away, or were thrown out. Often these kids vent their anger in destructive or self-destructive behavior — vandalism, promiscuity, drugs.

These kids become adept at using or manipulating people. ''They have to,'' one worker explained. ''It's a way to survive in a world they see as them versus me.'' These kids are the transients of the child welfare system; they bounce from one placement to another. They are the cogs of the machine called life in care, which has its own terminology: ''foster home,'' ''group home,'' ''specialized group home,'' ''outside

placement institution," "treatment center," "super-
vised independence unit." But whatever the name, the
reality is that the kids in care receive that care from
people who are not their family; their "families" are
paid workers. Love there may be, but there has to be
money to make it work. In the end, a lot of kids leave
the system. But, like people who have done time
behind bars, the kids become dependent on the system or institution to provide for their needs. A childhood spent in care is not a good passport to the real
world. One girl said, "We are whores in the system.
The social workers are living off the avails of public
money, the kids are getting fucked, and no one really
wants to know. They just want to hide the problem."
These kids will find it hard to get past grade ten; they are
learning disabled and they suffer from developmental
lags. Their energy has been spent not on intellectual
development, but on learning to protect themselves
at home.[1]

Imagine being a six-year-old child and being abandoned by your parents. Then, at ten, being taken back
home. Then being put back in a foster home. Still you
believe your parents want you. After all, they did take
you back once before. So you go home on a weekend
visit, and your parents call the social worker and say
they don't want you back again. So you go back to the
foster home, but now you can't fit in. You feel you are
being torn away from your parents. One boy said, "I
have been in four homes in eight years, and five different schools, so I have only had time to make enemies."
These kids say that social workers just prolong the
nightmare. One girl said, "I sure as hell do not trust
the social worker. She never told me what life would
be like in care; she never told me that I would be

exposed, with almost no privacy.'' Another commented, ''No one knows what it's like to have the label CAS over your head. They put us into homes where no one really wants us, where the people hope we will leave tomorrow.'' One kid said, ''I had some friends, and when their parents found out that I was in children's aid, they didn't want their kids to see me any more. I went into care to be loved, and I got treated like shit.'' Many of these children say they would change the system so parents who foster want to do it because they like kids, not just for the money. Child welfare workers would make surprise visits to see what is really going on.

Sabrina, eighteen, is bright and attractive. But at school, her performance is not up to scratch. Sabrina depends on impersonal sources of aid. Other kids have a family. Impersonal aid is not as forgiving as a family. Second chances are not always available. Sabrina is one of two sisters who come from an unstable family. Her parents fight. Her first placement was an emergency foster home, which she loved. But after nine months she had to leave. The children's aid needed the bed. Sabrina went through eight foster homes in less than a year. The children's aid tried very hard to get a suitable placement for her, but Sabrina wanted to get back to the emergency foster home. Being bright, she knew just how to break down a placement, often within forty-eight hours. She would be destructive. She would find the foster parents' weak spot. In time she found a foster home that accepted her. (Her fame had spread; some foster parents refused her.) But she has taken a beating, emotionally and mentally. Her schoolwork leaves much to be desired.

Two brothers who left home at different times are

in care. The older one, John, was subjected to physical abuse from his mother. Then he was kicked out. ''Only my mother reversed the story and said that I had run away.'' John's stepfather tried to intervene, but the mother was a liar, and very tough. One weekend John slept at a friend's house and called the CAS, on the advice of his friend's mother. ''My main worry was being sent back home. The CAS must have talked to everybody because even my school principal was there. My mother said I was too much of a burden, that I was a thief and a liar, that I had my own direction and no way was she going to have me back.''

The process was not fast. John was in court four times in six months before his case was resolved. John was lucky: he had three good social workers. It is interesting to hear how he describes his present worker: ''She puts her trust and faith in me, she listens without making judgments, and she helps any way she can. I feel she is there to help me. Her confidence makes me feel confident.'' He thinks a lot of social workers do not have the training to deal with kids. As for foster homes, ''Some are good and some are like jails,'' John said. Right now he is in a group foster home. ''Verbally they are my parents because I have been here so long, but psychologically they are not, because they can't give me the same support.''

For John's brother, the transition was not as smooth. He stayed at home a year longer, to make sure his sisters were all right. ''I wonder how I took it for so long,'' the brother says. ''The physical and verbal abuse. I didn't know what to do; I had no way of changing anything.'' There came a point when he could not take it any longer. ''One morning I was expecting a thrashing from my mother, so I left the house and went looking for my brother.'' He found John. Then the hard part began. ''They were going to send me home. I had to start fighting the system.'' Eventually he got a social worker and stayed in care. He moved from an emergency home to where his brother lived. Now they live apart. ''I got sick of the system. The household where my brother and I were living was run in a totally ridiculous way. The people were in it for the money. They would kick kids out because they didn't like them.''

John's brother has strong feelings about the children's aid: ''They are supposed to speak for the kids, but they don't. They don't have any idea what it's like to be in care, in a group home trying to survive on the money they give us.'' (In Toronto, CAS teens get $416 a month, plus $46 for a Metropass. That's $5,544 annually. The poverty line for a single person in the city is $11,080.) But, like John, the brother has high praise for his social worker: ''She is concerned about kids. She wants more money for them. She listens and is unbiased and doesn't push. My first social worker forced me into situations where I would rebel, sitting me down in a room and taping our conversation. I told him I didn't want him to do that, and I ran out of the office. So I got this worker, who I have had for four years. She is the one who really helped. I talk to her about my problems, and she is the only one who knows all about my past.''

A third boy, Ken, was not abused or maltreated, but his adoption broke down. He had been adopted in the sixties, into a family with two natural children. It did not work. The parents tried hard to make it work. They tried private schools, therapists, different living environments. ''You name it, they tried it, anything they could," Ken says. "It just didn't work out. I bucked it all the way." Ken left, "Something I wanted to do at age nine, and managed at thirteen." He went into care. It was not all he expected. He went to a group home with girls and boys. "That was good for me. It gave me a dose of reality. I learned that I didn't have it so bad. I also found out I wasn't such a bad kid, either." The big difference to Ken was the social workers: "The good ones listened. The bad ones and the ones who have been around too long tell you, 'This is what you need.' And I am saying, lady, you're talking crap, this is not what I need. I want to be heard, not told, I don't want to deal with some worker who has a neat plan she thinks works because she has been in the game for twenty-five years." Ken did get a good social worker. It took four tries, but he found one who listened and gave him support.

Care is a last resort. Many kids who come into care "go from hell to hell," as one placement worker put it. It is a scramble to find a placement, let alone an ideal setting. The ideal would be to assess a child over a six-week period. Most agencies do not have the staff, time or facilities to do that. Even if an assessment were made, it would be difficult for the agency to find the best placement anyway: again, the facilities are not available.

In her book *Children in Long Term Care*, Sally Palmer stated that the separation of a child from his or her natural parents is a traumatic experience and should be carried out in stages.[2] The child's name should go on an alert list when it seems likely that the child might be apprehended. This would give the child welfare agency time to line up a suitable foster home, introduce the child to the foster family, talk to the child about leaving the natural family, and muster the necessary resources to make the transition as smooth as possible. Palmer also recommends that the worker create a bridge between the natural and the foster parents, between the old home and the new.

It doesn't work out that way. Children are hustled into any placement that is available, and then they wait until the legal details are sorted out, which can take months or years. Meanwhile, the children move from emergency-receiving to assessment to foster home.

The back of a restaurant on Dundas Street East in downtown Toronto. A steady stream of police, construction workers, teenagers, taxi drivers, people with no fixed address or visible means of support, people the cops know well. They all eat the cheap, filling food. Some kids sit around drinking Cokes and coffee and smoking. They are explaining what it's like to be in care. "I had no idea what was going on," Steve explains. He's a thin kid, eighteen, sporting an expensive leather jacket and cowboy boots. He is out of the system and on his own and not doing too badly. He has a job, a place to live. He shares a room with his girlfriend, who was once a runaway. Steve lived on the streets and finally in a foster home. "There was a lot of booze and drugs going down in my family. My dad, he just fucked off, and my mom, she had a few boyfriends. Some of them were pretty rough on me. They weren't too easy on my mom, either. I was a problem kid in school, that's what the teacher said, a problem child." Steve looks around and starts to laugh at what he has said. "A seven-year-old problem kid. Boy, I sure was, I was hell, man. I think it was the teacher who blew the whistle, because the children's aid came in and got me and my sister. Jesus, was my mom mad at the children's aid. She shit all over them. She screamed and yelled, but it didn't do a lot of good. Man, I was history, gone, taillights in her life. But I had no idea what was going down, what was a foster home. No one told me why I was being pulled out of my home, either. I guess I know now. One of my mom's friends was trying to have it off with my sister or something.'' His friends nod in agreement.

Steve says they asked him what he wanted. ''I didn't know what the fuck I wanted. How the fuck could I? I wanted to go home.'' Some officially appointed professional asked him a lot of questions. He ended up first in a house with some other kids. ''They weren't bad, but I got the feeling that I was second best, that the family's kids came first. I guess that's natural.'' He went to another home, a permanent placement. ''There were kids so screwed up in that home, I don't know how that family managed. They were like fucking pretzels, bent. That's what one of my mom's friends used to say. He was English, from England. He used to say, 'He is bent like a pretzel.' So were these kids.'' He stayed until it became too much, and the foster parents had had enough.

Steve went to another placement. ''My social worker said they tried to keep me and my sister together but they couldn't find a suitable home for both of us.'' He pauses. ''I went to an old home in the east end. Near Coxwell. They had a couple of kids of their own, a boy and an older daughter. She was out of the house, at university. The son was still at home, in high school. The old man, he worked for the TTC, repairing, fixing street cars, like the old red rockets. They were good people. If it wasn't for them, hell, I would probably be out on the streets ripping off cars or something. They treated me like one of the family. I almost got used to calling them mom and dad. I used to see my real mom occasionally. She would come over to the house, and we would talk. She would tell me how she missed me and my sister, how she hoped we would all be together. I used to cry afterward. But I knew it was all bullshit, that we would never be a family again. I would never have a house to go to other than my foster parents'. My foster parents were really good people, they gave me everything I needed, and I think they really cared for me. But they are not my family, not my real family. They can't be.''

''You're right,'' says Amanda. Blond, intelligent and doing well. ''I beat the system,'' she says. ''Well, I had a little help from my friends.'' She laughs. It's obvious that the others admire, perhaps envy her. She is a winner, and many around the table feel they might be losers. Amanda was sexually abused. It was subtle. The mother drank. She was bored and angry, and the marriage was falling apart. The father saw his daughter as replacing the wife, in all respects. (A not unusual scenario in the lives of sexually abused children.) ''I took care of the house; I took care of my mother when she was incapable, which was often; I took care of my father. I slept with him. We didn't make love, but he did everything else. At first I didn't know if it was wrong, but as I got older I realized that it was wrong, very wrong. I knew I should not be doing these things. But who do you tell? The first person I could think of was my guidance counselor.''

That was just the start. ''Suddenly there is this social worker, with a cop. My father comes down to the school, and it's awful. They tell him what I have said, and he falls apart. Then he gets really angry and talks about lawyers. He says I'm lying. You learn fast that adults lie." Amanda was taken out of her home while her case went through the judicial system. She had to face her father in court and give evidence. (The father was charged, but agreed to counseling and was given a suspended sentence. The parents have since divorced. He wants to see his daughter, but she does not want to have anything to do with him.)

For Amanda, coming into care was the beginning of the anger and pain. "I went into a specialized foster home, one that took in girls like me who had been sexually abused. But having told about my father, having gone through the exposure, I suddenly became all screwed up. I became unmanageable. I felt the whole fucking world had betrayed me, especially my mother, who just stood by and let it happen." (Often, the mother knows, but is too frightened to intervene; she is afraid either of losing the husband, or of being physically assaulted.) "And my father used me," Amanda says. "He took away my childhood. I felt guilt. I felt used, dirty. I felt that the only way to get any love was to sleep with a guy. As far as I was concerned, all adults were liars. My first placement was a disaster. The family did not really like me, and I hated them. I felt they were playing head games — you know, isn't her case interesting? As for the social worker, I felt that she was studying me for some paper she was writing, that I was a neat case, which she would go back and talk about with her colleagues. I remember telling her that she was a bitch, a lying bitch, who didn't have a fucking idea what I was going through, and didn't care as long as she could use me." The social worker left. Another came in. Amanda was moved to another home.

"The next home was better. They were not using me. They didn't lie, and they didn't make a big deal about me being part of the family. They just let things take their course. But when it counted, they were very supportive, especially the mother. She used to hold me when I cried myself to sleep, and she never lost her cool when I screamed and yelled and swore at her and everyone else. I once tore my room apart in anger at my father, and she just said, 'We better clean it up.' No lectures, but she listened. That was the best thing, she listened. And I got a good social worker, who also listened and didn't make judgments. I wasn't just another kid in care to her, I was a person. She made a real difference. But I still haven't got a family, I'm not a normal teenage kid. I'm different. And the more I read about sexual abuse, the more I know that it's going to take a long while before I'll get over it."

When we left the restaurant, it was late. Winter darkness was settling over the city. Not far away, some teenagers were going home from school. They were laughing. They had the look of well-fed, well-loved kids, kids with homes to go to — nice homes, not violent or indifferent ones. Those kids belonged. They had relationships they could share, parents, friends, school, clubs, the social network most of us take for granted. They likely would not be thrown out onto the street when they reached the age of eighteen.

Life in an institution can be terrifying. Dean has just left a foster home. "Some homes are like jail," he says. "Foster parents need to be trained." Another young adult said: "The worst aspect is that I have ended up with such a negative attitude about the children's aid because of being in care. My sisters were and still are at home, and the children's aid asked me if they should be removed. I said no. Out here, every day is a struggle to get by. At least where they are, they are assured a roof over their heads and food. I do not want to see them in a home because of the way it is run. Once I was going to write to the newspapers to get this place closed down, but then I realized, if it was closed, where would we go? One thing, though, my social worker from the children's aid has opened doors for me. She has been a great help. What I am angry about is the foster homes, not the social workers.''

There is another group of kids, kids who are now leaving the system, at sixteen, eighteen or twenty-one. (The age at which you leave depends on whether you are still receiving some support from the system, whether you are still in school, and what status you have under the Child Welfare Acts.) Many kids who are older than sixteen need a temporary home, a shelter. They are not street kids. Many are still in school, trying to make it in a city with very little low-income housing. Most are trying to escape untenable family situations, or have been told to leave home.

There are only a few youth hostels, like Bethel Home or Etobicoke's Youth Without Shelter. (It is the only one located outside the city core.) Though five youth hostels are slated for Toronto — four in the suburbs — getting approval will take time. Few residents in the suburbs want a youth hostel in their area. (One father said that a hostel would make it easier for his son to avoid his responsibilities at home by giving him an alternative place to live.) North York's mayor, Mel Lastman, says, ''There aren't any runaway kids in North York, no homeless kids.'' The truth is that Mayor Lastman has a hard time accepting the truth about the most densely packed area of Canada, the Jane-Finch corridor, where there is abundant poverty, racism and the kids who need help. No suburb wants hostels for kids. Although he prefers commercial development, Mayor Lastman put his considerable power and prestige behind the setting up of a youth hostel in North York. (It could still take some time before it becomes brick and cement; it took a task force two years to find a site.)[3]

East of Toronto, in Scarborough, there is a proposal for a $2.5 million forty-bed youth shelter, to be called Second Base. It is intended for kids aged sixteen to twenty-four who have had to leave home. The project has the backing of church groups and most local politicians, including the local alderman, Kurt Christensen. (Of the three hundred new kids Covenant House receives every month, thirty-five are from Scarborough. Many of them are between sixteen and twenty-four, and are in a never-never land: they are too old to get help under the child welfare system, but too young for welfare.) The hostel was to be built on a vacant piece of land on Kennedy Road, south of Eglinton Avenue.

But the reaction of local residents was hysterical, often close to violent. One meeting ended when the police arrived, as opponents screamed and yelled at supporters of the shelter. (As the meeting ended, six kids from Scarborough were going to bed in a hostel downtown, and ten more were trying to find a roof for the night in an adult hostel.) ''I support youth today. I just don't want the shelter in my backyard,'' said one resident. The residents jeered anyone who supported the shelter. They were convinced the shelter would lead to vandalism, drugs and prostitution. Two thousand people signed a petition against the hostel.

Christensen, sensing the way the wind was blowing, did a fast turn, and is now helping to fight the project. Metro's manager of hostel operations, John Jagt, said: ''The idea hit the area at a time when the fears about the Scarborough rapist were high. As well, there had just been a murder in a transition home. The people could not see the difference between a transition home and a hostel. They are people with real fears. And it is not as if it were an old house that is going to be renovated or rebuilt. It's a vacant piece of land, so any structure will have an impact on the community.''

The shelter's opponents mostly occupy single-family homes, and they are victims of the so-called crime-wave hysteria. They are convinced that the shelter will bring horrors to their neighborhood — their daughters will be raped, their houses robbed. The hostel will have stringent rules and regulations, curfews, and staff, but that doesn't seem to make any difference. (The kids living in the hostel will be under tighter control than the residents' own teenagers.) Jagt suggested that the hostel workers could make the controls even tighter, to satisfy the neighborhood: an earlier curfew, fewer kids, say thirty or thirty-five, a change in clients, so that most of the clients are teenagers.

But people fear teenagers. Neighborhood residents think teenagers cause problems — drugs, crime, rebellion. They wear frightening clothing. Some people just can't understand why kids want to leave home; others think the kids should be given a bath and put in the army. Sixteen-year-old Allison Potts went to the Scarborough meeting, and told the hostile audience, ''I'm not going to vandalize your homes or molest your children. Youth are your future. Just give us a present." But the residents could not accept that the kids who would use the shelter had been abused or thrown out of their homes, or left because of violence, drugs or alcohol, and were too old to come under the care of the CAS. To the homeowners, the kids were skinheads, junkies and hookers. In the end, Scarborough City Council approved the proposed shelter, despite continuing threats from opponents.

One woman I know is on several committees set up to deal with youth. One committee is trying to establish a hostel for kids in the woman's neighborhood. She described the deep prejudices and fears about teenagers: "Here we are sitting around a table, discussing how to get the hostel off the ground, where to find a site for it, or a building that can be converted. Then the chairperson turns around and says, 'I don't want it in my neighborhood!' That gives you some idea of the obstacles that have to be overcome."

If a child is a Crown ward, which means in permanent care of a child welfare agency, with no hope or plan to go back to the natural family, then the child welfare agency will continue to support the child until the age of eighteen. That support includes room and board at a residence approved by the child welfare agency. In addition, the child gets a spending and clothing allowance. Approximately half the kids in care in Canada are Crown wards. After eighteen, the youth can still be supported if he or she is attending school. But to get funding, youths must be very good, with an excellent track record in care and at school. One lawyer told the story of two of his clients, who were taken into care and promised by the CAS that they would be supported until they were twenty-one if they were in

university. They were betrayed. The CAS stopped sup-
porting one at age sixteen, the other at age eighteen.
(In Edmonton, Alberta, only twenty-seven young people in care qualified for support after age eighteen in
one year.)

Those children in care who are not Crown wards,
who are voluntarily in care, who are non wards, or who
are society wards, are cut off when they turn sixteen.
Joyce Turnbull, associate executive director of the
Ottawa-Carleton Children's Aid Society, explains:
"These are children that we feel are likely to be
reunited with their families. That's why they are not
in permanent care as Crown wards." That's the hope.
But, as the child welfare agencies admit, very often the
hope does not become a reality.

So what happens when the child turns sixteen? "We
try to put them in touch with community services that
can help them, like welfare agencies or counseling services," says Turnbull. Student welfare pays $316 a
month, and there is a shelter supplement of $159. It's
not enough, especially in high-rent urban areas. And
only those kids who are in school get it. For those kids
who are not in school, eighteen is the age of majority,
and eighteen is also the cutoff. They are on their own.
"We would try to support them with counseling,"
Turnbull says. "But we do not have that many
resources to do it, and the youth also has to want it.
Many are distrustful of authority and institutions. They
just want to be on their own."

Under the law, each different age group is seg-
regated, by definition and by available resources.
Many agencies do not like to deal with kids who are
close to whatever age it is that puts them out of reach
of the child welfare system. One lawyer said, "I know

of cases where the child was close to turning sixteen, and the CAS would not intervene. Especially kids who fall under the Young Offenders' Act, who end up in detention before their trial because there are no beds for them anywhere. The CAS doesn't want to know.'' Beds are in short supply, and if a child is fifteen or fifteen and a half, there is very little time to work with him or her. The resources are better spent on a younger child. Yet until they are eighteen, children cannot apply for welfare, unless there are special circumstances — even if they are thrown out of the home. The General Welfare Assistance Act only applies to people eighteen or older. To get welfare you must prove you are eligible, and one of the requirements is a fixed address. The only way to fight the situation is to sue your parents — not an easy thing to do if you're out on the streets. "These kids can't make decisions about their lives, even though they are making decisions every day on the streets," says Diane Bergs, of Justice for Children.

There is even less support for kids who have left the child welfare system. Keep in mind that most eighteen-year-olds are not on their own. A Gallup poll conducted in 1984 showed that eighty percent of eighteen-year-olds were still at home.[4] But some eighteen-year-olds do not have family or friends. The contact with the social worker usually ends, and, because the children have lived in several different homes, they have had little opportunity to find friends who shared the same experiences and problems. The differences between a young adult leaving the family home to find his or her way in the world and the young adult leaving care are vast. The first child knows that, if it all falls apart, he or she can go home. Such children usually have numerous personal possessions, which can be used to equip a new home — radio, stereo, television. Often the parents will help with furniture and other household necessities. If they get an apartment, Mom or Dad can always provide references. These young people have what so many take for granted — a fixed address, a place for phone calls. These youngsters most likely have networks of relatives and friends. (Most kids, when they move out, go where they have friends, a job or school.)

Eighteen-year-olds coming out of care have none of this. They might also lack social skills, personal ambition and job discipline. "We have to learn budgeting, how to buy food, get a bargain, how to run a household, where to pay bills, how to use a bank," one eighteen-year-old explained.[5] Many of these young adults end up on some form of welfare. And their backgrounds often add to their problems. Most of the kids in care come from a background of poverty — inadequate housing, family instability, health problems, low educational achievement. It would take a mighty effort and a perfect system to enable children in care to overcome all these handicaps, then be able to face the world without any support.

Too many children leave care with low educational skills and are unprepared or ill equipped to get employment. Many children go from child welfare services to training schools to prison.[6] Some of them die. Ricard Cardinal's history is not one the Alberta Social Services Department will be proud of. The boy had lived in twenty-eight foster homes and institutions since he was taken into care at age three. Then, in 1984, a few months before he turned eighteen, fearing the care would come to an end on his birthday, he hanged himself between two birch trees. His death led to the appointment of Herb Sohn as Alberta's children's guardian; his role is to monitor government care of children. (Sohn was formerly with Children's Services of the Ontario Ministry of Community and Social Services.) Sohn admits, ''There is a need for after-care services in Alberta, but right now the main effort is taking care of children in the system.''

Three years after Cardinal's death, another eighteen-year-old was cut off from the child welfare system. According to people who knew him, he was scared of growing up. His foster mother said, ''He was emotionally delayed, suffered low self-esteem and lacked many of the basic life skills.''[7] He ended up at a party near Grand Prairie, where he was badly beaten, then drowned in a pond. The night he died, he was drinking and taking drugs. He was unable to cope without support. And the professionals have no way of knowing what will happen to children after they leave care.

Fay Wilson says, ''These kids are being socialized to be the underbelly of the next generation, and I am supposed to fix them up in six months.'' Wilson is angry. She runs the Pape Adolescent Center. It's a large, rambling house in Toronto's east end. It's not a residence, it's a support service. Its objective is to prepare kids for the real world once they leave care. The kids who use the service are between fifteen and twenty-one, and there are about two hundred kids a year. The center has a staff of eight. ''We will work with them as long as they want to work with us,'' says Wilson. ''Once these kids leave care they have no supports, so if they don't have it together they could end up in dire straits." It's not easy, and these kids have to be more ready than other eighteen-year-olds. Most of them have to become adults before they're ready. "A good slice of these kids are never going to be independent in ways that society wants. They will end up on the streets, in jail. Of the rest, well, we are pretty over-stretched serving them," Wilson explains.

The center needs money, partly because the Ministry of Community and Social Services, which funds the center, increases its grant by four percent each year, while staff costs go up by at least eight percent. The result is that the center loses staff. One girl who uses the center said, "It means we won't get as much help as we could. I found out that there is not enough money to get another worker. If we lose a worker who isn't replaced, it's like we're stepping backward. These people are all trained professionals who are here to help us, and if you guys keep taking them away, who will help us? We're going to be on the streets, high and dry. I don't see what $30,000 is compared to what the staff do for the kids. Believe me, from the bottom of my heart, if there are not services for kids coming out of CAS, there is gonna be a lot of lost kids."

The kids who use the center need help. They are not used to making decisions. Many of them have had at least four decision-makers in their lives at all times, from social workers to foster parents. The attempt is made to save them — but with limited resources. And sometimes the workers have to make some hard choices. A young girl in one social program was hooking, and the decision was made to throw her out of the program. The choice was made after the staff had spent a lot of hours and a lot of emotion trying to turn the girl around. "Freda," the supervisor told the girl, "we're here to prepare you for independence. We're here to help you make a life for yourself. We are not here to keep you in shape for your pimp."

It was a traumatic experience for both sides. Freda saw her social worker almost as a mother. The girl was badly damaged. She was owned by everybody, sexually and emotionally. Her pimp was her uncle. Her sister had been killed two years earlier because the uncle had found out she was hooking. Freda's idea of a date was to give sex. But her program was helping to give her a sense of identity. She was treated like a person who had control over her life. People who know her say she has a brilliance when it comes to working with handicapped kids, that she has a great deal to give to society.

Scarborough, Ontario. Tucked away in one of the more pleasant residential areas is a large five-bedroom house, equipped with every convenience: televisions, microwave ovens, VCRs, stereos. In today's market, house and contents are worth at least half a million. But this is not your ordinary house. It's a residential program run by East Metro Youth Services. Like the Pape Adolescent Center, it has a mandate to get kids ready for the real world, the world beyond care. In the house are six kids with a range of problems. Two are big boys, more than six feet tall, and prone to anger. "The key is to defuse the anger before they get out of hand," one house staff member explained. No mean skill, when faced by some kid who has a lot of bitterness caused by a life history of sexual or physical abuse, or who has been dumped off on the CAS without any explanation. "If you can't stop it, just let him go, let him pound out the walls. They know the consequences. They know they will have to pay for the damage. So try something else, go outside, go for a walk."

These kids have been through some form of treatment facility; they've had serious behavioral problems in school. Now they're at the end of the line. One worker says, "We have to teach them some basic social and life skills, things like how to write a résumé, how to budget your money, how to cook, all the skills that in a normal family they would have acquired." There are a lot of these kids, but very few agencies want to know about kids older than eighteen. At eighteen, a person becomes part of the adult system. But often these kids are not adults. They are socially retarded, still trying to work out who they are. They are kids in adult bodies, and they have no place to go.

Most kids come into care at age twelve. Four to six years later they hit the streets, and most will not make it. Once again they will end up as throwaways, only this time the cost to society might be a lot higher. It takes $60,000 a year to keep someone in a penitentiary. For many of these kids it's the logical final chapter of their lives. Others hurt themselves. These kids are called slashers. When they are disturbed or angry, they slash themselves, cut their arms or ankles. "They say they are angry," a social worker explains. "They want to get rid of that anger. They say they feel compelled to cut themselves; then the anger will go out of them. Most say they feel very calm after they have cut themselves. It seems as if they are cleansing themselves."

Another program is the Life Program, where kids live

in a residence in what is termed "semi-independent living." The on-duty staff members live in and act as role models. The rules are strict, and school is a must. The Life Program houses five girls. There are two residences like this in Toronto, one for girls, one for boys.

If you listen to these kids, you get a sense of almost desperate insecurity, of a world of changing rules and residences, of never really knowing what will happen. Continuity and predictability are words that have little meaning for these kids. How predictable can life be when your parents want to get rid of you? These kids have been betrayed too often to trust. One boy described it this way: "I'm in a sort of foster home, just me and their kids. They treated me like a family member. I try to play that down. I don't want to get attached again. I don't want to get into the fights I had with my parents. I put up a barrier." A girl added, "I think all the time, my parents didn't want me, why would my foster parents want me? I do not want to get hurt like that again." Another said, "Why should you trust foster parents when you don't even trust your real parents?" One girl said: "I had a social worker who I really liked and trusted and opened up to, and she left without telling me. I had another one, and I'm talking to her and I'm crying and she looks at her watch, says 'That's too bad,' and walks away. You phone them and they are never there. To them you're just part of a caseload."

Part of a caseload, a number on file, a name in a computer. No say about what happens in your life. In harsh terms, when a child is taken into care it means that an agency is assuming control over the child's life. Social workers, agents of the system, will take over.

No matter how good the system, the underlying premise is control. Once the system moves to protect the child or act in the child's best interest, then a child's welfare becomes the business of Child Welfare. The paperwork and files build up, the computer screens glow, meetings take place. The child becomes an object with a cash value. How much per diem? What can we afford? How many workers can be spared? The child is a management problem, in need of strategies and objectives. A terrifying number of people are involved: police, lawyers, social workers, doctors, psychologists, lawyers, teachers, all working for the system, all with an interest. All are trying to do their best, but the best does not seem good enough. If the system were good enough, there would not be so many kids coming out of care who are not making it, who end up unemployed or behind bars.

Because the system leaves much to be desired, an organization to help kids in care or who have left care started three years ago. It's called Youth in Care. Youth in Care is one project of the Canadian Child Welfare Association. Its president is John Meston. Youth in Care was started by Troy Rypstra, then a nineteen-year-old who had been in care for six years and decided to start this network. It's patterned after a British organization, the National Association of Young People in Care, an advocacy group for the eighty-six thousand youths in government care in the United Kingdom. The group provides kids in or just out of care with a network support system, and lobbies for better services for kids in care or coming out of the child-care system. One youth in the program, Dallas Nickoli, a twenty-one-year-old former Alberta government ward, explained, "I'm interested in seeing that youth have a stability in their lives, that they are not just dumped out into society when they reach a certain age. I want to initiate some independence training programs and to change the image of youth in care as being juvenile delinquents."[8]

FIVE

Saints, Devils and Social Workers

It's been a bad day for Miriam. She's a children's service worker with twenty-eight kids in foster homes, group homes, special-treatment foster homes. Some are doing just fine, others are not. Some kids have problems — they've been badly scarred by emotional, sexual or physical abuse. It's Miriam's job to try to save these kids: to support them, to sort out their problems. When a kid who has been taken from his or her family faces the problems of becoming a teenager, the kid's anger and feeling of being betrayed come out, and the kid ends up "in conflict with the law."

Today Miriam has been putting out fires and, as she says, "wondering why the hell I'm doing this." Her job isn't made any easier by what she calls the bullshit — the endless flow of paper, the lack of support from supervisors. One of her cases is a girl she managed to help. The girl was a hooker; now she's winning awards in school. And she's getting married, but the agency won't kick in a few bucks for a wedding present. The phone rings. Wearily, Miriam picks it up. It could be another disaster, some foster parent who needs her help to sort out a kid who has acted up or run away. Or a child who is going through some crisis instead. It's one of her clients, Sandra. She's calling now to say she hadn't seen Miriam in a couple of weeks, and missed her. ''That,'' said Miriam, ''made me feel a hundred percent better. That's when you realize that you're doing something worthwhile.''

That's Miriam's world. It's not neat and tidy. It's messy, as all human relationships and emotions tend to be. She's the back-up hitter in the child-care game — only it isn't a game. Lose Miriam's influence and you may have a human time bomb walking the streets, or kids unable to cope, hold a job, be a good parent. With twenty-eight kids, Miriam has to make some tough decisions. Which cases should she concentrate on? Which ones can drift a bit? She must hope and pray that her assessments are right. Now she's spending a lot of time with three kids, all of them in rough shape. One girl was sexually abused, and now the family wants her back. But the parents are alcoholics, and the CAS has recommended that the girl stay in care. ''I love that kid,'' Miriam says. ''We have put a lot of work into her, counseling, group counseling. I knew she needed me a bit more than the other kids I look after.''

Another child was abandoned at the age of three months. The mother disappeared. The child was made a Crown ward and stayed in care for fifteen years. All that time there was no word from the mother. Suddenly the mother showed up, wanting to be reunited with her child. Miriam has to act as a buffer. ''The child is in emotional turmoil. Out of nowhere comes this woman who says she's the kid's mother, and she expects the kid to love her, and the kid feels guilty as hell, because he is supposed to love her, after all, it's Mum, but he doesn't. I sit down with him and say, 'Look, it's important to see her, get the hurt out of the way, find out why she left and why she came back.' ''

Every day there is the nagging worry. Miriam asks herself if she is making a difference. Is she helping, or is the work she does only as effective as a Band-Aid on a cancer patient? The answers are few and far between — the kids that phone and say hi.

If effectiveness is measured in time spent with each client, the mathematics are against Miriam. Too many cases, too few hours, too few resources. At most, she might be able to spend an hour and twenty minutes with a client each week. But even that is hard. The demand for reports and more reports chews up her time. She does a lot of the paperwork on weekends, but still her time with the kids is eaten up.

Like Miriam, family service workers do not have enough time. These people work directly with families who have kids in temporary care or who need help with kids at home. They carry caseloads of up to forty-five families. If one family needs a lot of counseling, the others have to wait. There are sometimes three weeks between visits to a family.

The daily diary of a child-care worker is a study in time management. There are team meetings, supervisor meetings, court appearances. Whole days can be lost. Then there are visits from clients, and travel time, which in remote areas, can add up to sixteen hours a week. And of course there are the ever-demanding phone calls. Time becomes a commodity to be hoarded. Overtime becomes endemic. That may sound fine if you're thinking of overtime pay, but in a high-stress, emotionally demanding job, overtime can mean a faster rate of burnout and a drastic lessening of attention, commitment and performance.

In Canada, the emphasis in child care has shifted from intervention (removing the child) to prevention (helping the family to cope). There are several reasons for the change. The first is the belief that the family should be preserved at almost any cost. The concept is deeply ingrained in all child-care and social welfare agencies. According to Professor Marilyn Callahan, all child welfare legislation has three things in common. "They are concerned with who will have custody and guardianship of the children; they reflect often minimal standards of care and behaviour permitted for children; and they define the process by which custody and guardianship will be changed if minimal standards are not met."[1]

But as Callahan and others have pointed out, the legislation does much more than that. It sets the rules and guidelines for child welfare workers, it defines their powers, and it reflects government's and society's views about children and the family. The acts also limit when the state can intervene in family life. In the Yukon, Alberta and New Brunswick, provincial legislation demands preventive services. In Quebec, legislation provides the child with the right to counsel. In Ontario, the Yukon, Alberta and Manitoba, the child may be granted legal representation. In most provinces, however, legislation says that an appropriate agency can intervene only after a child has suffered some harm and has been perceived to be at further risk. (The exceptions are New Brunswick, Quebec and the Yukon.)

Professionals who have looked at the legislation say the change from intervention to prevention came out of a feeling that the professionals were not to be trusted. In some cases, the professionals were made to look incompetent. People began to think that, if any-body is to be believed, it should be the family. This attitude was reinforced by a long list of problems with various children's aid societies, especially in Ontario. The result was legislation that implied that child wel-fare agencies were poor substitutes for parents who were struggling. The legislation contains a series of checks and balances, which are preserved by the courts. Judges look askance at child welfare agencies that interfere in the life of the family. Social workers know that, in most instances, the courts will side with the parents. The social workers and child-care agen-cies must gather evidence that will stand up under the scrutiny of the court. This is especially true in cases of neglect, a hazy area.

Unfortunately, in the real world of child care it's crisis management, rather than prevention, that pre-dominates. At the same time, there are not enough resources for children who are taken into care or who are in any type of temporary wardship. Often it is less expensive to leave children with the family — the roof is in place, the bed is there, the maintenance is at hand. "If you apprehend the children, what are you going to do with them?" a social worker asks. "The foster care system is underfunded, and it's breaking down. We're sending kids from Toronto to Owen Sound." In the push to keep the child at home, the front-line worker looks for a relative, someone who can take the child in.

One case has become part of the folklore of the chil-dren's aid. During an apprehension hearing, the judge asked the mother who the father of the child was, thinking the child might be left with its father. The mother knew only that his name was Joe and that he hung around a particular pool hall. A worker takes up the story. "So the judge orders the social worker to find the father, and off this poor, young, new, green social worker goes. She finds the pool hall. She goes in and asks, 'Is Joe here?' Well, there are ten Joes! What Joe does she want? 'The Joe that met this lady, Cindy, and dated her, and they got very close. . . .' 'Close,' they ask, 'how close?' 'Well,' she says, 'close. . . .' She never did find the Joe who got close, and the kid was taken into care. But it shows how anxious the courts are to keep the kid at home."

The child-protection legislation appears very progressive in its attempts to find the least intrusive alternative for the family. But meanwhile, how can social workers protect the children? There is very little money available, and as the number of abuse cases rises, the workers' ability to prevent abuse drops. Thus the workers must create priorities: which cases, for how long? Most social workers prefer to work with their clients over long periods, or at least spend "meaningful" time with them. To avoid taking kids into care, professionals need to work with the family before there is a crisis, when there is less stress. A worker explains, "The families you can get to early are the ones who call up, who ask for help or for a temporary placement of the child. But those are the first to go when you are pushed for resources. The flip side is that, if you don't put kids into care, by the time you have to do something, the kids are really a mess. I have kids who want to kill — or want to kill themselves."

In Canada, more people are beginning to report child abuse, and the reporting laws were changed so it is now mandatory for professionals to report suspected child abuse. (If they don't, they are fined and reported.)

And the number of reported cases of child abuse — especially sexual abuse — has increased dramatically. As a result, there are hundreds more kids who need placements, treatment, specialized facilities. At the same time, more parents are asking for help, but there are no more resources. The caseloads mount up, and the social workers and other people involved in child welfare are under more stress.

In St. John's, Newfoundland, the incidence of reported sexual abuse skyrocketed by seven hundred percent in a little more than a year. It was becoming apparent even to the most calloused that something had to be done. In March 1987 a Child Abuse Treatment and Prevention Unit was set up under the Department of Social Services. The supervisor is Marilyn McCormack. The unit operates as a front-line intervention team: they do the initial investigations, sort out who needs what, plug people into available services. They also co-ordinate the assessment of the children. The unit carried a number of ongoing cases, and its files are growing. ''We need more workers, more facilities. Two-thirds of our cases are sexual abuse, which takes a lot of energy and time to handle,'' says McCormack. In a province with chronically high unemployment, the stresses on families are great. And, McCormack explains, ''Stress leads to a lot more abuse of kids, and to wife beating. I guess we are no different from any other area of Canada.'' The problems and frustrations are the same, as well. From sea to sea, child welfare is low on every politician's list of priorities.

According to child-care professionals, the child protection system is overburdened, and the workers' cases are becoming more complex and difficult. The kids are tougher to deal with. Many people think one reason is that they are left in crisis situations for too long. One child-care worker commented, ''By the time they are pulled out, or by the time it gets serious enough for the child-protection agency to intervene, the kid's in real trouble. It's not prevention, it's salvage.'' As well, there is increasing demand for accountability. Workers are hemmed in by procedural regulations. In British Columbia, according to some observers, if a service is not directed at a child in danger, it isn't funded. Money is spent on specialized services to help kids who are badly damaged, but there are few facilities, especially foster homes, for kids who just need a loving environment. One worker called it ''the industrialization of child care.'' Social workers today process information. They gather it, analyze it and enter it into a variety of decision-making machines — computers.

Many social workers feel they have lost control. The computer is everywhere. The computer is efficient. But efficiency and effectiveness are not always the same thing. ''When you are dealing with human lives,'' says child welfare consultant Barbara Chisholm, ''with disordered and complicated people, you have to be inefficient in order to be effective. Cost-benefit analysis and computers tend to force the social worker, the professional practitioner and the client to fit the system, rather than fitting the system to the people.''

The system. Child-care workers hate it. Once a system is in place, once a hierarchy is established, flexibility decreases. Workers learn to minimize risk and avoid making decisions. It's not the best way to run a child-protection service. One worker said, ''I got burned out. I was there for six and a half years, and at least half that time was spent surviving the system. After a while I said to myself, I just can't do it any more. I could deal with the clients, but it's dealing with the rest of it, the bureaucracy, that burns you out.'' Other workers are more explicit. ''We have eight hours a week for client contact and twenty-seven hours a week to cope with the bullshit,'' they say. They all agree they could be more efficient if they could delegate some of the mundane clerical jobs. One of them said, ''A week ago I saw that my secretary had nothing to do. I had a kid, fifteen years old, who had been in care since he was two. Suddenly the agency wanted to know if this kid had certain immunization shots. I spent a whole day trying to track down the kid's doctor. My secretary could have done that — but no way. Any time I give her a job like that she gets hell.''

The Children's Aid Workers Union, the Canadian Union of Public Employees and the Ontario Public Service Employees Union claim that one-third of CAS front-line workers suffer from burnout. It's been the subject of several studies, one by Robert Mcfadden of the University of Toronto's School of Social Work. Mcfadden said that inexperienced and inadequately trained workers are particularly vulnerable to burnout.[2] After eighteen months on the job, a worker either quits, falls apart or survives for another eighteen months. Most workers claim they can tell within three months who will last.

> For the newcomer, in addition to constant mental and physical fatigue, it means discovering that there is no time to plan, to think, to prioritize, to prepare, and evidently, no time even to feel.[3]

In British Columbia, Alberta and Saskatchewan, cut-backs in social services have had a demoralizing effect on child welfare workers. A family court judge in Edmonton said: ''They [child-care workers] have been demoralized for a number of years; they are over-worked and under a lot of pressure just at the time when the government is cutting back resources. How bad is it? Well, at Christmas a kid was being horribly abused. The kid was referred to the local child welfare branch. They were shut down for two weeks for Christmas. How could you shut down social services? In Alberta, it's easy. It saves money.''

British Columbia completely eliminated its child-abuse and neglect-prevention programs in the name of fiscal restraint. The director of the Professional Social Workers Association, Chris Walmsey, noticed a lack of graduates willing to enter the Ministry of Human Resources. ''They will take lower salaries rather than the uncertainty of working for a government that has a record of firing social workers,'' he said. The government cutbacks have led to high turnover rates and a greater difficulty in hiring staff with professional credentials.

The cutbacks have created a dilemma for workers, who must try to work within a system that is constantly demanding optimum solutions in the best interests of the child yet that provides no money. But how do we define ''the best interests of the child''? Who makes that judgment? Who is the worker representing, the agency, the child or the family? The lines are obscure, the mandate unclear. Yet whatever workers do, their attempts to deliver the best service are affected by the lack of money. Workers try to find assessment homes, foster homes or group homes, or places in mental-health clinics. They shuffle kids from one place to another constantly.

Experienced social workers have harsh criticism for the training new workers receive. There is too much theory and too little teaching of what child protection and child abuse are all about. The schools are beginning to realize the shortcomings in their academic programs. But money is in short supply, and budget constraints limit what the schools can do. Some schools in Calgary and Victoria emphasize child welfare, and attempt to bring native Canadians into social-work programs. Many schools do not, and blissfully operate as if nothing has changed, or ever will.

Some social workers have noticed that there has been a shift away from the skills of social work — that is, interviewing and how to listen — to clerical skills, primarily how to manage systems. Many people think university schools of social work are not sure where they should be heading. Like all academic institutions, they must choose between what society needs, what the government wants and what practicing graduates say is required. Most universities believe that a Master of Social Work (MSW) is sufficient training for the job. They argue, with some conviction, that they provide a theoretical basis and some practical experience and that an employing agency must do the in-house training. The universities also think the agency should provide management training, which is not taught in the university courses. But there is very little time and there are few resources for in-house training. Most workers attend the Front Line Worker course at the Ontario Center for Prevention of Child Abuse, sponsored by the Ministry of Community and Social Services. But workers don't take the courses during the critical probationary period of their career.

Another problem with the university programs is that they forget there are two Canadas: the rural north and the rich south. The outlying northern areas face often insuperable problems, and workers must deal with Native Canadians, long distances and lack of facilities. Academic training at most universities does not acknowledge these differences. Like everything else in Canada, child care can become a victim of geography. The farther from the big southern cities and metropolitan areas, the lower the workers' academic qualifications and the fewer the number of specialists. Some northern areas, like Sudbury, are fortunate to have a community college that can produce a community social worker and a university that awards a Bachelor of Social Work (BSW). But most remote areas are not well served. Salaries are lower, conditions are harsher, and caseloads can be grim. Abuse, alcoholism and poverty are rampant in many parts of northern Canada, our rural slum, as some call it. These problems put additional strain on front-line workers, who must counsel families as well as supervise the children. Most northern and rural areas have trouble hiring and keeping staff.

The policy of keeping the family intact creates as many problems as it solves, and it places additional burdens on workers. They must spend more time with families, supervising, counseling, helping. Many agencies have established community co-ordinators or child-abuse co-ordinators. These co-ordinators try to make the community help provide resources; they also lobby various groups within the community to help protect kids. One community co-ordinator described her job: ''I go into a high-risk, high-need area and try to build networks. For example, if the family needs certain resources, I and the case worker will try to identify what is needed, and it's usually the same things that come up: day care, housing. Instead of working individually with the family, we try and get the community involved, to create community solutions.''

To do the job properly takes commitment, time and persistence. Co-ordinators must work with tenant advocacy groups, day-care advocacy groups, women's organizations, service clubs — any groups in the community that can contribute to protecting children and helping families survive. Co-ordinators are involved in developing protocol, and they help write procedures for co-operation with the police and with other organizations, such as schools.

But what is the role of the child-protection worker? Workers are told that the interests of the child are paramount. At the same time, they're told, with equal vigor, to keep the family together. Workers can sometime lose sight of the child while trying to help the family. The conflict between protecting the child and protecting the family has never been resolved. The agency that removed your child then tries to help you resolve your problems.

Who are the child-care workers? We don't have a lot of information about them. But we do know that more than seventy percent of child-care workers are women, and most of them are in their mid-twenties. Slightly less than half are married. (The number of women in social work has grown dramatically since the 1960s, when there were equal numbers of men and women in the professions. Now eighty percent of social workers are women.) Most child-care workers come from middle-class backgrounds, and often their training does not help them understand deprivation or poverty, which they haven't experienced. One child-care worker was a victim of physical and sexual abuse. She described a class she was taking. "I looked around and I saw all these nice kids from nice two-parent families from nice neighborhoods. They hadn't had to live on mother's allowance. They had no idea of the fact of poverty, of what happens in not-so-nice not-so-middle-class families. When we discussed sexual abuse and physical abuse they freaked out. They did not believe such things happened."

Professions that are dominated by women have hidden problems. By chance or design, governments tend to underpay women workers. Workers with equivalent qualifications in other parts of the civil service, such as teachers, are paid more than social workers. Workers with fewer qualifications but greater political clout, like police officers, are also paid more. Social workers' salaries have not even kept up with inflation. Women are not found in great profusion in the upper ranks of the child-care system, despite agencies' and governments' affirmative action programs.

Workers will also attest to another fact of life: children have a low priority in any government's agenda. Society at large does not place a great value on children, and that attitude is reflected in government spending. The first programs to get cut back are the social services. Perhaps not all provinces are as brutal as British Columbia or Alberta, but the result is the same. Less money, fewer workers, decreased morale and increased turnover of staff, which can be as high as thirty-five percent annually. Like a rat on a treadmill, the child-care worker keeps running to stay in place. There are few back-up people to cover staff who are sick, who want to attend training courses or who are on vacation. Frustration levels rise.

As well, while workers feel increasing pressure and emotional commitment, there is little support from those farther up the chain of command. This is not to condemn all child-care supervisory staff: the majority are dedicated, and support their workers right down the line. The morale, efficiency and stress felt by the front-line worker are in large part a reflection of the supervisors, and their ability to support and communicate with the worker.[4] A critical factor is how the worker thinks the supervisor represents the field workers to the administration. As well, supervisors do not always understand how the workers feel. For example, it is never easy for a worker to apprehend a child. But supervisors are not always aware of the stress a worker feels in apprehending a child. The tension between supervisors and front-line workers emerges in the cynicism of workers. Many workers feel supervisors let them down.

Good social workers can relate to people and listen. Both are good management qualities. But can the supervisors manage? Can they make tough decisions? Do they back up their people? In the end, compromise is the path to supervisory success. One supervisor noted, ''We don't want dynamic leaders who will make tough decisions. After all, a wrong decision doesn't mean a fall in profits — it could mean a child seriously injured or dead. Better compromise and caution.''

Child-care workers deal with poverty, alcoholism, abuse, mental illness, frightened and angry kids and bitter parents. They see kids who have been burned, beaten, thrown against walls, hit with hammers, sexually assaulted. They see kids who are emotionally disturbed. They see thirteen-year-old hookers, and boys turning tricks. They face the wrath of parents. Child-care workers have been punched and threatened with knives and guns. Some people call them ''baby snatchers.'' They work with people who are overwhelmed by poverty, who do not have a decent place to live, who are unemployed. When the child-care worker arrives, these families face one of the greatest crises of their lives: the possibility of losing their children.

Social workers know that there is no time to help these families. When some parent calls up and pleads to be taught parenting skills, a worker might be able to spare two hours a month. Court cases, paperwork, emergencies, committees and the worker's thirty other cases take time, too.

The result is burnout. Unless workers change jobs occasionally, most will burn out within two years. Burnout is especially fast for child-care workers because they see the worst realities of the human condition. The child-care workers' problems are increased by demands that are often impossible to meet. Continuous long-term exposure to stress can lead to personality change and psychological damage, or something social workers call ''institutional dehumanization.'' Every child-care worker has a story of a colleague who folded up, who could not get work done on time, who moved from excuses to lies and evasions, who finally started to break down when confronted by a supervisor, and realized the job was not worth the sacrifice.

When a worker suffers from burnout, the clients are badly served; if the worker quits, the clients must adjust to a new worker.

Other workers might try to put distance between themselves and the client. This is not the pursuit of objectivity, a necessary component of a social worker's armory, but a growing cynicism. Workers develop a negative attitude toward the client, talk to and about the client as if he or she were an inanimate object, and withdraw from contact. Such workers take refuge in going by the book; they become mechanical bureaucrats, devoid of creativity or compassion.

The stress, the increasing paperwork, the lack of resources, the need to cajole, fight and argue with committees to get anything done — all these are taking their toll on management-worker relations. The first confrontation took place in June 1977 when Catholic children's aid workers walked out for twelve weeks. Since then there have been more strikes; in 1986, for example, five children's aid societies were on strike.

Society wants to believe in the dedicated child-care worker who is willing to cope with pressure, strain and burnout to keep the system going. But the myth of the dedicated worker is being replaced by the reality of the militant and angry worker, who believes that society's expectations are too high and the system's rewards too few.

SIX

All I Need Is a Bed

First child-care worker: I don't think we have lousy foster parents. I think we have good foster parents, if we use them right.

Second child-care worker: Maybe. But I have kids who have gone through forty different placements. . . .

Third child-care worker: Kids are placed in foster homes who should be in treatment centers.

Second child-care worker: Some foster homes are good, but some are horror stories.

Third child-care worker: If we get a good one, we abuse it because we overuse it.

First child-care worker: When we find a good foster home, we'll put three or four kids in there, because we have to place those kids somewhere.

Not too far from downtown Toronto, on a side street, there is a group of three-story town houses. In today's market, they are worth more than two hundred fifty thousand dollars. One is for sale. Inside, the house is warm and comfortable. There are bookshelves with volumes on sociology, social work and psychology. The kitchen is small, tucked away near the front entrance. The woman who owns the house, Sheila, makes coffee and explains that the house is an assessment home for teenagers.

Sheila is abundantly qualified to run an assessment home. She has a university degree and a wealth of experience, both in Ontario and overseas. After working at Toronto's Clarke Institute of Psychiatry, Sheila started doing assessments of troubled teenage kids for the CAS. That means living with them around the clock for three months. She does her job well, but she is getting tired. One reason is that there should be twelve assessment facilities for the Toronto CAS but there are only eight. The assessment home must be willing to take in kids with emotional problems, sight unseen. The kids who live at Sheila's house are not cute TV teenagers. They are manipulative and often cunning. They have had to be, to survive. Dealing with these kids requires skill and an infinite amount of patience and understanding. Sheila has to be a bit more manipulative than the children are. Relief from the teens' incessant demands is not easy to find.

"I do it because I'm crazy," Sheila admits. "Most of the time I enjoy my work. As I get older, I get a little more tolerant and a little more objective. I realize I can't change the world. I go to therapy, because I need the support. If I want to take a weekend off, I would have to hire someone to take over, for one hundred and sixty-five dollars. But who in their right mind would take this responsibility for that amount of money?"

She outlines a typical day. "Nighttime is the worst; darkness brings back the terrors. I get to bed around midnight, and am up at six making breakfast. No going to school on an empty stomach. At breakfast we discuss the day ahead, medical appointments, personal needs. Then, when they get home, I spend about an hour with each talking about their problems and how they are going to handle them. It seems there is always some crisis — at school they have gotten into a fight, or they are upset. In the evening we work on social skills.'' The list of commitments and demands seems endless, and I wonder how anyone could cope. Normal parents have a hard enough time with their normal kids. And Sheila's rewards are few: "You add up all the little things and that's the reward, that's what's important.'' The kids at Sheila's are fortunate. They have a placement with a qualified social worker. Not all kids are as lucky.

The need for beds. That's the system's euphemism for shelters for kids who have been taken into care, for whatever period of time and for whatever reason. There are not enough beds to go around. At every level of the child welfare system, in almost every jurisdiction, for every kind of shelter, there are not enough foster parents.

Who becomes a foster parent? Two studies have been done.[1] Most foster parents begin fostering in their mid to late thirties, and take in about fourteen children in six years. They are married, and live in the city. Often neither parent completed high school. Usually the father is a blue-collar worker, and the sole wage earner. The father's income is about $29,000 — well below the Ontario average of $41,775. (Most middle- and high-income families do not choose to foster, perhaps because, in a large number of those families, both parents are working, and they do not have the time to foster. As well, they might not think the income from fostering is worth the physical and emotional costs.) This profile seems to be universal. A British Columbia study, carried out in 1987, shows a remarkably similar profile.[2]

The studies and statistics do not convey the raw

human side of fostering. One foster parent called it ''the blood, toil, tears and sweat of fostering, when you cry with the kids, laugh, watch them succeed or see them fall apart, become street kids and end up like their parents.'' Statistics can't describe the foster mother who stays up all night comforting a child who is crying because he will never see his mother again. Why do they do it?

For a lot of foster parents the rewards are small, and the physical, emotional and financial costs are high. Many are leaving the system. The shortage of foster parents and foster homes is critical in most of Canada's urban areas.

According to the Ontario Association of Children's Aid Societies, the number of foster homes has decreased by seventeen percent since 1981. The number of kids in care has decreased by almost the same amount. But the number of beds available has dropped much more dramatically. Because of Ontario's housing crunch, people cannot afford large homes, and the number of available beds has decreased by forty-eight percent. Small agencies serving rural areas have an oversupply of beds. Different social and economic conditions prevail in rural areas — only one parent working, bigger homes with more space, a closer knit community. One of the reasons for the dearth of foster parents in urban areas is that new parents are not being recruited. Existing foster parents are the best recruiters, but they are not doing it. Most feel they are not getting the support they need from the child-care system. (The largest children's aid society in North America, in Toronto, has exactly one person assigned to recruit foster parents.)

The crisis in foster care is not new. A decade ago I wrote, "The harsh reality is that across Canada there is a desperate shortage of all types of foster homes. In Metropolitan Toronto, for example, nine hundred foster homes are needed — three hundred are actually available. And the number of foster homes in Ontario dropped twelve percent between 1973 and 1975."[3] As expected, when any government-supported agency has a problem that might require money, you have a study. In 1979, there was a discussion paper, "Foster Care." That led to a policy statement, "Standards for Foster Care," in 1985. Between October 1981 and May 1982, there were discussions involving the community, the child welfare agencies and the Ministry of Community and Social Services. In 1984 the ministry released another report, this one called "An Analysis of Foster Care Practice and Structure In Ontario." Then came a joint effort from the Ontario Association of Children's Aid Societies, the Ministry of Community and Social Services and the Foster Parent Association, called the Foster Parent Project, from 1983 to 1986. There was another report in 1987, called "Partners in Care: Exploring Health, Burnout and Support Dimensions of Foster Parents." The Foster Parent Association carried out its own membership survey in 1985. In May 1987 the Ontario Association of Children's Aid Societies launched the Residential Care Research Project, which it called "The Future of Foster Care." In its first report, the project acknowledged that Ontario's foster care system was approaching a crisis of major proportions.

The tensions come at a time when strains on foster parents are increasing. Because of the present emphasis on keeping children at home, when they are removed for their own protection, they are in bad shape; many have severe problems.

> The child in foster care today may have come into care after extensive and extended protection services have been provided to his or her family. He or she will be more likely to have been abused and a candidate for Crown wardship. He or she will most likely be suffering from severe emotional trauma and be exhibiting behavior problems requiring skilled management.[4]

The foster parents agree. "Ten years ago," said one, "the children we received were a lot younger with very few problems. Now we have older kids coming in who have a lot of emotional problems, teenagers who have never had their problems resolved." Another said, "A lot of times, by the time we get the child it's too late. The kid's got a lot of problems." Another was more explicit. "Under the present rules we only get the most difficult cases. We are looking after some very aggressive acting-out kids, which we never had before." Before, these kids would end up in a specialized foster home, one that gets more agency support and money. But these kids have to have a bed.

Much of the problem was caused by provincial governments who were seeking ways to cut social spending. This led to the policy of "deinstitutionalizing" child care. (The same thing happened with mental health care.) "Deinstitutionalize" is a word developed by the bureaucrats, who sit comfortably in offices far removed from the realities of how a policy is translated into a reality. The policy was not developed simply to save money; much was a sincere and often correct belief that institutional care was not the ideal. People who were cared for in institutions ended up divorced from the community; they were often unable to cope outside the institution. So the bureaucrats decided to send them to non-institutions — and what better place than foster homes? It's a lot cheaper. Unfortunately, we are now seeing the bureaucratization of foster care; we are slowly moving from the volunteer amateur to the volunteer professional. Today foster homes range from the "specialized adolescent foster home" to "group homes for the retarded" to the "view-to-adopt foster home." (By definition, a foster home cares for four kids or fewer; a group home takes in four or more.)

They look neat and tidy on paper, all those specialized foster homes ready to cope with all those emotionally wrecked children. In reality, foster parents are expected to salvage these children, and they are not getting particularly well paid for doing it. Most are walking a tightrope, with the natural parents on one side, the children's aid on the other. And the children now have a lot more rights than before — and they know it. "When those kids come to the foster home they have their little booklets on their rights. But what rights do we have as foster parents? What discipline can we impose? It takes a lot of patience and understanding. A lot of people can't cope with the new rules — so they quit," one foster parent said. "These kids have more rights than my own kids have," added another parent. "You can end up running a two-tiered system in your own home if you're not careful. And don't think your own kids don't pick that up. They'll ask, 'Why do they get away with this or that and I can't?' ''

The increasing demands being put on foster parents, who have to cope with difficult children with serious emotional problems, have, by accident, not by design, begun to create a two-level foster-care system. On one level are the ''mom-and-pop'' homes, run by people who see themselves as an alternative family for the child in care, and who are motivated by a desire to help. On another level are the ''professional'' foster parents.

Few of the ''mom-and-pop'' parents are motivated by the financial rewards of fostering; many of them do not have a complete grasp of the system of financial compensation. Many of them take in foster children to follow their church's teaching that they should help the less fortunate. (Their sentiments are in sharp conflict with the yuppie hedonism of the eighties. Charity is not the long suit of the baby boomers.) These people believe that making the foster child part of the family is the most important part of fostering. ''They — the two boys — are part of our family,'' one foster parent explained. ''They are treated just like our daughters and son. We go out together, go camping together. We are a family.'' These people have a repertoire of practical skills; they are stolid, firm. They rely on common sense. Their children are self-reliant. These people resist the drumbeat of professionalism that is beginning to sound throughout the foster-care system, especially as foster parents are pressured to deal with ''troubled'' children. To the traditional foster parent, common sense, firmness and love are more important than degrees or books.

But in the mom-and-pop homes, there is a growing sense of unease. The foster parents think they are being used by the system. They are angry because they are not highly regarded by those they serve, the child welfare agencies. The foster parents feel they are not trusted, consulted or respected. One foster parent said, "We need recognition for what we are, what we do, for the level of intrusion into our family. Fostering is not valued. People see foster parents as people who cannot do anything else." Another parent adds, "People do not understand the role we play or what we do. Social workers see us as glorified baby-sitters, at least the young workers do. And because we don't have a degree, they think we aren't qualified to help make decisions about what should be done with the children."

This feeling of being left out of the decision-making is echoed by many foster parents. Jackie Jordan tells the story of one young girl. The children's aid had been worried that she would be sexually assaulted by her stepfather, so they put her on the pill. The girl was removed from her home, but somehow the mother got the child back. Jordan says, "I told the children's aid she should not go back home, but she did. In the end I was right. The stepfather raped the younger sister, and there were signs that the mother was incestuous with the younger brother. The children's aid did not believe the older sister. I told them, you believe what that child says." If the children's aid had listened, a tragedy might have been avoided.

The moral? Trust and partnership. Easy words to pronounce, and standard vocabulary of the child welfare agencies. But it's only lip service.

Many foster parents have voiced the need for greater

agency support. In an ideal world, a child welfare agency would have a separate unit responsible for foster-care services. The unit would supervise outside placements, foster care and adoption. The ideal agency would also have a foster-care resource person, who would carry a caseload of foster parents and act as the link between the agency and the foster parent. The resource person would be a source of support, and might do everything from assisting with the child management to setting up some relief for the foster parent. One study recommended that a resource unit be created to supervise foster care, adoption, outside placement institutions, agency-operated foster homes, parent model group homes, volunteers, family support programs and psychological and medical services.[5] All these services would be centralized, and would have their own organizational structure, staff and objectives. Some agencies have adopted this model in whole or in part, and have had success with their foster parents. They regard the foster parents as part of the team.

Unfortunately, the ideal world comes bang up against the real world of few resources, little money and inadequate personnel, heavy caseloads and crisis management. There are the eternal problems — social-worker turnover, burnout, changes in job classifications, too much demanded of too few, large caseloads. All these problems affect the foster-care system. Few agencies can afford a social worker who works with the foster parents; even those few are overworked. The foster parents want a weekly telephone call and a monthly meeting; often the agency can't provide that support.

The foster parents who do get the agency's attention run the specialized foster homes. There has been an unplanned but continuing shift from mom-and-pop foster parents to "professional" foster parents, people who are trained to cope with the damaged child. Some of them see fostering as a career that allows one of the parents to stay at home yet still earn an income. According to a 1988 study, "The Future of Foster Care," these people received greater support and training from the agencies.[6] They felt they were part of the child's treatment team. They also received more money than other foster parents, and the added income reinforced their view of themselves as professionals. They are confident and capable people who take their job seriously. Slowly, by unstated policies and unfolding practices, the foster-care system is becoming professional. The reality might not match the image we like to hold of the foster parent, that of a loving, generous, unselfish amateur, ready to volunteer.

But it means better training for foster parents. Agencies must weed out parents who have an idealized picture of foster parenting, and provide courses on how to deal with damaged kids. Foster parents today are trained in child development; they look upon fostering as a career. Volunteerism is on its way out, and a new, more practical system must be put in place. The new system will be based on cash. Foster parents will be properly compensated for what they do, and there will be more money for more social workers to support foster parents.

That's what's needed. What we have now is a reflection of society's interest in children, and of government priorities. The Government of Ontario, for example, is prepared to spend only $319.20 per month to support a child in a foster home. That is less than the cost of renting a parking space for a month in Toronto's financial core — $350 — or boarding your pet dog — $360. It is true that the government will pay to cover out-of-pocket expenses, called "reimbursables," such as prescription medicine, clothing, bus fare, and birthday and Christmas presents. The government's recommended rate for these expenses is $5.19 per day. (As one foster child noted, that "gets you into a movie, but no Coke." But then again, why should a foster kid be able to go to a movie?) And a few agencies pay a subsidy, as well, which can be as high as $4.91. The average daily subsidy paid by the agencies in 1987, however, was $3.09.

The average basic board rate for a child in a specialized foster home is only $21.62. These are homes that deal with damaged kids, kids with problems who require extra effort, understanding and patience. They deserve more money. But as every child services worker will point out, in the urban centers, the mom-and-pop foster homes are saddled with damaged kids, yet they are not getting the extra money. Foster parents also must worry about property damage, and they fight constantly with agencies to get damage claims settled. (Most insurance companies will not pay for damages done by children in foster homes.)

Just what are foster parents? Sue Hamilton of the Ontario Ministry of Community and Social Services says, "They are not employees. They do not have a pension plan, even though they might have been fostering for twenty years. There are no employee benefits." Foster parents come cheap — too cheap. No benefit package, no union bargaining committee, no gold watch, nothing. Yet many foster parents do not want to lose the altruistic volunteer element; they do not advocate a system based on financial rewards. Many foster parents do it by choice; they are prepared to give much and receive little.

Yet the role of the foster parent has changed. Governments and society cannot rely on the good intentions of a few to take care of the many. The few are willing to volunteer for whatever task society needs accomplished for the common good, and by their volunteering they become exploited by the majority, who place greater and greater burdens on them. "In the end," one foster parent said, "we are being exploited right out of the system." Foster parents must decide if they want to become full-time professionals, with the resulting demands for more accountability, paperwork and bureaucracy, or remain underpaid but overworked semi-volunteers, semi-professionals. One person who worked for the Catholic Children's Aid Society said, "We have not begun to compensate these care givers in any way for their time, their skills, the level of demands we have placed on them or the physical, financial and emotional risks that they undertake in providing care for our children."

The foster parents of Metro Toronto have demanded a basic rate of $26 a day, plus expenses. The ministry offered only $23.69 a day, to include expenses. This represents a hike of $1.50 a day, or 6.8% — about a nickel an hour. Joe McReynolds, a ministry spokesperson, explains: "Fostering is a volunteer occupation; it has not been seen as a job." He adds that the ministry is "examining the issue" — in other words, buying time. But time is running out. The foster parents went on strike and refused to take in any more children. With 160 kids arriving at Metro's child welfare agencies each month, the agencies had to scramble to find beds.

Thirty kilometers north of Toronto is a town called Mount Albert, a combination of new developments and old rambling homes. The house on the corner of Main Street looks like any other, except that it is surrounded by a chain-link fence, and the yard is full of equipment for kids to play on. The house is a foster home run by Rita Bonner. Along with her husband, she has been taking care of kids for twenty-five years. Four years ago he died, so she is carrying on alone.

Rita's charges all have problems. Some have Down's syndrome, some have other forms of mental retardation, and some have other severe physical or mental handicaps. These kids cannot be left alone to look after themselves, and for Rita, every day is long. Sometimes one of the kids, Jamie, will thrash around all night, trying to break the bonds of a straitjacket he sleeps in. Without the restraint, he would hurt himself. Every day is laundry day — six loads for the seven kids. And Rita makes the meals and drives the kids to medical appointments. (The driving alone costs her $250 a month.) Fostering is a constant emotional and physical grind, but Rita says she loves her kids. She says she could make a lot more money as a psychiatric nurse, a career she is trained for. But she hangs on, out of a sense of commitment, loyalty and love.

Rita is on strike for more money. She wants to keep the system going, but she wants the system to acknowledge that what she does is worth something, has a value in the terms our society judges people by:

hard cash. Rita cries when she talks about working so hard. Her love is turning to a bitter anger because she feels betrayed by a callous government. She thinks the ministry probably ran a poll, looked at the results, translated that into votes, and quickly realized that, in today's world, foster parents, their cause and their kids don't amount to much. And the anger is spreading to other parts of the province. In Ottawa, the number of foster parents has fallen from 700 eight years ago to 284. The remaining parents want to double the daily rates for fostering.

Ironically, the demise of the traditional foster home might lead to a reliance on privately run institutions rather than volunteer foster homes. In Ontario, children's aid societies, like mental health centers, have community boards. The province funds private agencies it feels will be around for a long time, but it will not fund profit-making agencies that provide children's services at the primary, or children's aid, level. There are some private facilities the children's aid socieities are allowed to purchase services from; these facilities are very tightly regulated.

Often these ''private facilities'' are privately run homes, both foster homes and group homes. They are called outside placement institutions, or OPIs, and they charge $50 to $85 a day per child. In 1976, eight percent of kids in care were in OPIs; in ten years the number doubled, to almost sixteen percent in 1986. Allan Stewart, the president of Stewart Homes, says, ''We get a lot of kids whose foster home placement has broken down, and a lot of kids who have been abused in the foster home.'' Ted Storey runs Storey Homes. He says, ''We are in business because there are not enough foster homes to go around.'' Both say that most of their kids do not need specialized care, and would do well in a warm foster home. But those beds are not available. The private group homes or foster homes have the staff and facilities to deal with the damaged child who cannot fit into the normal foster-care system. Because they are private and depend on the children's aid society for clients, they must do their job well.

But if there is not enough money to properly compensate foster parents, where is the money coming from for the far more expensive private foster homes? Are children being placed where the dollars are available? Or are they placed in a home based on what they need?[7] Children's aid society workers will tell you that they start off looking for the best placement for the child; then they look at what is available. Often what is available is a private placement, an OPI.

The scramble for beds is growing, and the shortage of facilities works against the child welfare agencies — and worse, against the kids. If the screening is not as good as it should be, if the follow-up is a bit sloppy, it is the child who takes the pain. It's the child who suffers until the shortcomings of the residence are exposed. In 1988, one headline read, ''Abuse trial hears of 'torture' at group home for teen-agers.'' The home was closed, and five employees were charged. Another headline said, ''Probe ordered into complaint against home.'' The house was a privately run group home for difficult teengers. The manager of the advocacy office at the Ministry of Community and Social Services acknowledged that there were too few places for young people who need specialized care.[8]

What do the child-care workers say? Some of them talk about the government study on foster homes, and some of the report's recommendations such as the one in favor of moving from the volunteer to the professional foster home. But they admit that would cost money. They think the government should do something about the foster-care crisis. A good place to start would be by collecting some data about kids who leave the system. What happens to them? Some workers theorize that children were a "sexy" issue in 1979, the Year of the Child. They say street kids are sexy now — hookers, boys hustling men, and so on. But kids in care are not sexy — the issue has no political appeal. The workers say the agencies have no kids in care, no standard diagnostic classifications. They point out that the lowest-paid workers in Canada are day-care workers. People who take care of children are not rated highly in our culture.

Will the children's aid survive? Can we afford to keep paying lip service to volunteerism, from boards of directors to foster parents? Will the idea of foster care survive in the big urban areas? Perhaps the government will begin to focus on non profit foster-care facilities. As the workers point out, non profit means a lot more government involvement. More money might be spent on professional staff or unionized employees.

Perhaps the child-care workers are right. But will a professional foster-home system be any better for the kids? We need to do some basic research, to find out what really happens to kids in care.

SEVEN

The Victims

Three in the morning. A seven-year-old boy lies in bed, awake. He stares at the ceiling in the darkness, waiting for the sounds from the next room to move from a rhythm of brutal invective to a cadence of violence. He's too tired to cry. Besides, it's been going on so long, as long as he can remember in his short life, and the bitter repetition has made him almost immune. The noise increases. Words tumble through the door and down the hallway. Bitch, whore, slut. . . . Then the sound the boy dreads, but knows so well, flesh hitting flesh. His mother crying. A chair is knocked over, a door slams. The silence is broken by his mother's sobbing. The boy tries to sleep, but fear keeps his eyes open. He knows that tomorrow it will be his turn to face the beatings, the sweep of his mother's hand clutching a broom handle, a belt. The sudden pain as his mother plays out her own rage and frustration on her son.

It's not always like this. His father, overwhelmed by a marriage he didn't want, emotionally drowning in a tide of business and personal problems, seeks the solace of Scotch and works out his bitterness on his wife's body and her soul, and she, in turn, moves down the path of stronger to weaker, and beats her son. The child will go to school and explain the bruises by claiming a mishap on the stairs, or roughhousing with some friends, even a fight. Tonight he will swallow his tears and hope that tomorrow night will be peaceful.

In his life, there is no one he can turn to or trust. It's an adult world, and his parents have made it clear that retribution will be quick if he tells anyone what goes on in his home. Pride precludes his telling any of his friends. And since he is well dressed, well fed, obviously from a solid middle-class home, what teacher would think he is an abused child? What doctor would look closely at the bruises?

A few years later, when he was thirteen, the child, a more confident boy, did unburden himself. Ironically, it was when he was applying as a junior counselor in training at a YMHA summer camp. One of the staff gained the boy's confidence. One day, while the two were alone in the camp office, the boy began telling his story about the beatings, the drinking, the violence. He did not tell everything, keeping the mother's abuse on the periphery, something that was important, but second in importance to the tension between his parents. The social worker listened, making the occasional comment. After all, this was a trained social worker, adept at gaining confidence and soliciting information. Two days later, when the boy went home, he was greeted by a grim father who berated him for lowering himself and bringing shame on his family, currying favor with the social worker by telling him stories about his life at home. ''You have betrayed the family, betrayed our trust.'' His mother warned him that she would deal with him, but by that time his size had precluded physical attack, and his mother had altered her strategy. She used subtle emotional abuse. Still, the boy was lucky. An uncle took the place of the father, and the boy managed to escape his home. Most other kids are not so fortunate.

A bold black headline on the front page of the Toronto *Sun*: "Two year old girl beaten to death." Charged with second-degree murder was a twenty-three-year-old man, Glen Wilcox. According to the police report, the child was punched and rendered unconscious. The child's family had moved into Regent Park, an Ontario housing development; they were said to be quiet and keep to themselves.

In St. Catharines, Ross McNab is given a sentence of six years for putting a five-year-old boy under scalding water in a shower. The incident occurred in Edmonton, but the child did not receive medical attention until four months later when the man, who was living with the boy's mother, returned to St. Catharines with the mother and child. The boy is left with permanent scars on his back and buttocks and the restricted use of his left shoulder as a result of the burns. Ross McNab's mother and father, a St. Catharines doctor, have documented their support for their son.

Twenty-nine-day-old Angelica was examined in a hospital, and was found to have had every major bone in every limb broken. "These injuries were deliberately inflicted," said Dr. Robert Bates of Toronto's Hospital for Sick Children. "I've never seen anything as severe and remarkable as this case," said orthopedic surgeon Edward Fink. He added, "One hopes one would never see this type of case again." One pediatrician said it was the worst case of child abuse he had ever seen.

Other children end up dead, as did Robbie Drudge, two and a half. Robbie spent his last weeks in a depression, mourning the fact that his mother had abandoned him. His depression took the form of refusing to eat; if forced, he later vomited or soiled his pants. In response, his guardians, his mother's brother, Rene Drudge, and his wife, Sharon, beat the child, by hand or with a wooden paddle. The end came when Mrs. Drudge screamed at the child for not washing his soiled pants. Robbie jumped back from the chair he was perched on and struck his head. In the next four days the child had fits, was unconscious, screamed, had his left arm paralyzed and stared as if in a trance. Mrs. Drudge did not want to take him to hospital — she was worried about being accused of child abuse. Finally, on Easter Sunday, she awoke to find the child had stopped breathing. What makes this case stand out is that the Drudges were given temporary custody for three months on the advice of the Catholic Children's Aid Society of Metro Toronto, who thought that the risk of giving custody to the Drudges was acceptable. Apparently the risk was higher then the CCAS was led to believe, for, as Sharon Drudge admitted, she hit the child so often her hand hurt, so she used a wooden spoon.

In fact the family, that cozy ''you me and baby makes three,'' is a myth. According to one sociologist, ''The family is the most violent group in society. You are more likely to get killed, injured or physically attacked in your home by someone you are related to, than in any other social context.''[1] One U.S. survey, done in 1975, showed that eight million women, children, wives and husbands were punched, beaten, struck, stabbed or kicked at least once a year. In any one year, the survey said, one out of every six couples will have some form of violent altercation, from knives to throwing a coffee pot. And the survey found that child abuse is 129 percent higher in families where there is also spousal abuse.[2] It was estimated that the same conditions applied in Canada. That was ten years ago. Not a lot has changed; the levels of abuse and violence do not seem to have receded. In fact, we have been hitting our kids for a long time, but like anything that is cloaked in the wrappings of "the family," admitting that children were being seriously injured took a long time to accept.

It took close to a century for child abuse to become public, to become an issue, even though the medical profession had for years been seeing evidence of the assault on children. Much of that evidence was collected in Paris in the 1850s. A large, broad-shouldered man whose face betrays kindness and intelligence is working in the Paris morgue. He is a doctor, and his specialty is forensic medicine. Ambroise Tardieu, professor of forensic medicine at the University of Paris, dean of the faculty of medicine and president of the Academy of Medicine in Paris, is looking at the corpses of children. He has noticed fractures that did not fit the stories he had been told by the children's parents or the police reports. His examination of children's bodies has led him to the conclusion that these children had been assaulted by their parents. In 1860 he published his findings:

> From the most tender age, those defenceless unfortunate children should have to experience . . . the most severe cruelty, be subjected to the most dire privations, that their lives, hardly begun, should be nothing but a long agony, the severe corporal punishments, tortures before which even our imagination

recoils in horror, should consume their bodies and extinguish the first rays of reason, shorten their lives, and, finally, the most unbelievable thing of all, that the executioners of these children should be more often than not the very people who gave them life. . . . This is one of the most terrifying problems that can trouble the heart of man.[3]

Tardieu's paper was acknowledged by his colleagues, but was ignored by the public. The industrial revolution was in full swing, and children were keeping the mines and mills running. Few people worried about working conditions for the children. Even children who were in school suffered corporal punishment. In the eighteenth and nineteenth centuries, people worried more about animals than children. Dr. Tardieu's discoveries and conclusions were discounted; people preferred to believe that the fractures were caused by rickets. After all, the good middle class would surely not beat their children to death. Dr. Tardieu was ignored; the medical profession's answer to his paper was silence.

The silence was to last a long time. There was not another mention of the abuse of children until in 1946, when Dr. John Caffey published an article on the topic. Caffey had examined infants who had bleeding in the skull, and found that many of them also had broken bones.[4] He knew the brain damage was caused by some form of battering. When he connected the brain damage with the fractures, he realized that the injuries were not accidental. He knew his discovery ran counter to accepted beliefs about loving parents, who acted in the best interests of the child.

But slowly the doors of silence were being pried open. Seven years after Caffey's discovery, Dr. Frederic Silverman of Stanford University and Dr. Astley in England were asking some troublesome questions based on separate investigations of children's injuries. Why were they seeing old as well as fresh fractures? Why were there bruises on some children's arms and legs? Why should there be blood in a child's vomit and feces? Why were some children undernourished? Why did they seem to thrive in the hospital, then quickly become sick again when they were discharged?

In 1953, Dr. Silverman published his finding in an article entitled "The Roentgen Manifestation of Unrecognized Skeletal Trauma in Infants."[5] (In lay persons' terms, The X-Ray Evidence of Unusual Bone Injury.) He concluded that parents who abuse their children do not recognize the symptoms; or, they recognize them but are unwilling to admit it; or, they may deliberately batter their children, but they deny it. Meanwhile, Dr. John Caffey continued to fight. In 1956 he gave the Mackenzie Davidson Memorial Address in London. His message: there is a need for the early detection of child abuse, so that children can be protected from further injury. A year later, he urged his fellow radiologists to stop ignoring their findings, and to start investigating any suspicious injuries to children.

Yet the message was not getting through. What was needed was a phrase, a slogan, something to grab people's attention, to make child abuse a legitimate subject. At the Colorado School of Medicine, Dr. Henry Kempe, a pediatrician (why did it take that discipline so long to find out what was going on?) was becoming concerned about a growing number of children suffering from mysterious injuries that did not appear to be caused by household accidents. With his colleagues, he conducted a nationwide survey of hospitals and attorneys' offices to determine how many of these "mysterious injuries" there were. The results were shocking. For every million children, 250 to 350 were being abused. Kempe's study concluded that physical abuse was a major cause of maiming and death among children. But he said members of the medical profession were loath to report or investigate abuse. From Kempe's survey came the phrase that would finally catch the world's attention: "The Battered Child Syndrome."

The place: an expensive condominium in Toronto. Outside, the city's skyline is etched against the evening sky. Inside are signs of success: tasteful furniture, classical art. The rooms reflect a sense of the good life. The woman seems to reflect the surroundings; she is tall, confident, successful. But appearances are deceiving. Behind the success and the money is a story.

Celia is a statistic. Here is her story.

> My father started abusing me when I was four. He used to come into my room to kiss me goodnight and tuck me in. He would fondle me, sort of play-tickle, but the tickles would lead to him gently rubbing my stomach and between my legs. Yes, it felt good; it was very pleasant, this gentle rubbing and fondling.
>
> My mother, I recall, was not a strong person. She depended on my father for everything, money, clothes. . . . She had no other life. She drank — not excessively, but she drank. Occasionally she used to go away to visit her parents. Then my father used to sleep beside me and spend hours fondling me. As I got older, it got worse. My mother lived in the

house with us but she was not a part of us, not a part of our lives. It was my father and myself, and his sexual desires became focused on me. He used to ask me to touch his penis, always saying that he loved me, and that it was all right. I guess I loved him. I *did* love him. He was my father, he took me out, he bought me clothes and toys, whatever I wanted. He could afford it; he was a very successful businessman. He had his own company, and we lived in a very large house, with a gardener and a live-in maid.

So I would do what he wanted. When I was about nine, he would kiss me all over. By the time I was eleven I was his lover in everything but name. There was no force, just the constant petting. He was very gentle. I felt like I was his special girl. I sometimes think it was like playing doctor in the garage, only this was real, this was real sex. It was all so damn easy, so inevitable that I would have intercourse with him, that I would let him fuck me. The worst part is that I liked it. I had become his wife. He would talk to me about the business. (I imagine that is why I took an MBA and went into business.) He would take me out for dinners at very sophisticated restaurants, sort of showing off his pretty daughter. I suppose by then most of his friends knew my mother was not an ideal wife; they accepted me as a sort of dinner substitute. And I would go to the theater or movies with him, that sort of thing. I believed that there was nothing wrong. Who was around to tell me? Not my mother. I was an only child. My father managed to keep me fairly cut off from my friends, though I did not realize he was doing it.

Then I hit puberty and went to high school.
God almighty, here were girls talking about
necking. Necking! I couldn't believe it! Was I
abnormal? What the hell was going on? I realized that what had been happening to me, the
relationship I had with my father, was a per-
version. It was wrong, totally wrong, and I was
just finding that out. The bastard had lied to
me. "It's all right," he used to say. "There is
nothing wrong. We both like it, we love each
other." But always he added, "Don't tell anyone." Our "love" was a travesty, a corruption
of family relationships.

I had no idea what to do. Do I go to my
mother? Who do I tell? Who will believe me?
Who will believe? That is all I could think of.
One day I blurted it all out to my mother. She
smacked me across the face; I thought she
would kill me. She began to yell, scream, cry.
She called me a liar, a whore. She said I had
seduced him, that I was a slut, that I was
making it up. She went back and forth between
calling me a liar and calling me a whore. She
said I was trying to take her husband away.
Then she said something I will never forget: "I
don't care if it is true or not, I don't care, but
if you ever tell anyone else I will say you're a
lying little bitch, you understand? Don't tell
anyone, because you will get hurt more than
he will."

I know she never told my father what I had
said because the situation remained the same:
the footsteps late at night, my bedroom door
opening, his soft hands. I was too scared, too
numb, too powerless to stop it. In the end I told
my teacher. I told her because I trusted her, I
don't know why, but I did. The long and the

short of it was that my father denied it all. He said I was lying, it didn't happen, I was making it up because I was angry at him. Then he sort of smiled and suggested perhaps I was a bit spoiled. His Bay Street lawyer was there, and he was a rich businessman. Who was going to believe me? I was well dressed and well fed; I had no physical scars. The children's aid would think twice about going to court against my father. And my mother wasn't going to say anything — no goddamn way. She needed the roof over her head and the money in her purse, and anyway I'm sure she believed that I took her husband away from her.

I think that the only thing that saved me was my teacher. I remember her holding me and saying, Celia, I believe you, I know you are telling the truth. But it didn't stop. My father wanted to go on as before. It became hell. He tried to control my dating, my friends, my life. He was jealous, very jealous. Then one day I grabbed a knife and I told him I would kill him. I don't know if he was scared — he was a pretty big man — but I think he realized if he kept on there would be physical violence, and he wasn't prepared to go that far. If I suddenly had bruises, he would have a tough time explaining them away. It would destroy his image. So it stopped. But it has never stopped for me. It has cost me two marriages. I have carried it around all these years, and it has taken a lot of time and energy to bring me to a point where I can start to deal with it.

I will never forgive my father. I refuse to see him. I know he has tried to contact me, but as far as I am concerned he is history. The bastard

stole my childhood. He raped me, plundered
my body, and my mind. He fucked me round,
that son of a bitch. Sometimes I wish I had
killed him.

In the 1950s and 1960s, after Kempe's study of child
abuse, the cumbersome machinery of government
rumbled into action. Child welfare laws were passed,
changed or tightened up. Child welfare agencies had
their mandates expanded. Reporting laws were over-
hauled and tightened up. No longer could doctors or
other professionals hide behind a wall of silence. The
definition of abuse was expanded to include deprivation and neglect, the denial of adequate care, and the
endangering of a child's life or morals.

But for many years sexual abuse was not included
in the definition. It was too controversial to deal with,
and many people could not even comprehend the idea,
which called into question every belief in the relationship between parent and child. Like physical abuse,
sexual abuse had been going on for centuries. In 1835,
for example, in Victorian London, four hundred adults
were living off the avails of child prostitutes, and
venereal disease among children was well
documented. One of the major accomplishments of the
Victorian child welfare agencies was to raise the legal
age for prostitution from nine to thirteen. But the few
steps taken to protect children from sexual abuse were
halfhearted.

Sexual abuse, like physical abuse, was detected a century ago, and again it was Dr. Ambroise Tardieu who
exposed it. In a book he published in France in 1878,
he referred to the alarming number of adults who were
accused of raping children younger than sixteen. Of
almost ten thousand cases, the vast majority involved

girls. Tardieu wrote: "What is even sadder to see is that ties of blood, far from constituting a barrier to these unpardonable allurements, serve only too frequently to favor them. Fathers abuse their daughters, brothers abuse their sisters."[6]

Tardieu pointed out what today's child-protection workers well know: that too often the child is too frightened to accuse her father. After Tardieu's book was published, there were several studies on the subject of sexual abuse of girls. Some doctors realized that sexual abuse does not always leave a visible scar, but the lack of a scar does not mean the abuse did not take place. In 1896, Paul Bernard, of the Faculty of Law in Lyon, looked at some cases of sexual assault involving young girls. Like Tardieu, he found that a large number of cases involved incest. He also found that a large number involved people with an education. Bernard believed the stories of the children he talked to.

Paul Camille Hippolyte Brouardel was Ambroise Tardieu's successor to the chair of legal medicine in Paris. He continued to study abused children, and he opened up the Paris morgue to medical students. Like Tardieu, Brouardel wrote about the violent physical acts committed against children by family members. Brouardel especially noticed sexual assault that ended up in murder.

But the growing body of evidence of child abuse was not to go unchallenged. The challenge began when Alfred Fournier addressed the Academy of Medicine. Fournier set out to unmask what he saw as the lies of the children who were claiming that they had been sexually assaulted. Fournier was a senior figure in the Paris academy, so his words had a certain credibility. They were words that males — religious leaders, conservatives, and the like — wanted to hear. Fournier said that children were not telling the truth. He wrote: "Girls accuse their fathers of imaginary assaults on them or on other children in order to obtain their freedom to give themselves over to debauchery."[7] Fournier also began the comforting theory — comforting for men at least — that women who are raped are predisposed to be raped. More and more medical academics were easily persuaded to espouse the "children lie" theory. One doctor, Claude Bourdin, concluded that children take pleasure in lying. It was easy to move from the "children lie" theory to believe that women lie, a belief that took more than a hundred years to alter. The abuser thus became the victim.

Sigmund Freud, who had been to Paris, was familiar with the two strains of thought regarding assaults on girls and women. From 1895 to 1896, Freud believed that his women patients were suffering because something secret and terrible had happened in their pasts. Unlike other analysts, he believed these women; he did not dismiss them as hysterical liars, the response they received from other doctors. Freud believed that they were revealing what had happened to them as children. Bravely, Freud published his theory. His paper was greeted with stony silence. His colleagues did not want to believe him. It was much easier to believe that the women were liars and were fantasizing what happened to them. In the end, Freud backed away from his findings. He chose to run with the hounds of conformity.

It would have taken someone with great courage to continue to argue against conventional theories. In his book *By Silence Betrayed*, author John Crewdson notes, "The last thing the fledgling psychoanalytical community needed in its struggle for respectability was for one of its members — and a Jewish member at that, in a city that had elected an anti-Semitic mayor — to announce his conclusion that the Vienna of Wittgenstein, Mahler and Schoenberg was a city of child molesters."[8] Freud wrote to his close friend Dr. Wilhelm Fliess, "Surely such widespread perversions against children are not very probable."[9] To support his new theory, Freud had to find some explanation for the "fantasies" of his women patients.

His search led him to develop his central thesis, which he called the "Oedipal impulse." Taking the Greek myth of Oedipus literally, Freud saw the suppression of illicit sexual desire as the natural outgrowth of maturation. The boy was in love with his mother, the girl with her father. They suppress their desires, and thus do the right thing. The children can then feel a sense of self-esteem.

When his patients talked of sexual relations they had had as children, Freud decided they were really talking about their unconscious desires for those relationships, and the desperate repression of those desires. His patients did not have sexual relations with their parents at all; they unconsciously wanted to.

Freud's failure is sad. But the good doctor was respected, and wielded great power in the field of psychoanalysis. Generations of psychoanalysts clung tenaciously to Freud's theory and resisted anyone who challenged it. A few, however, did find the courage to challenge it. One was Sandor Ferenczi, a brilliant Hungarian analyst and one of Freud's closest colleagues. Ferenczi reluctantly began to accept that some of his patients were sexually abused as children. More alarming, they admitted they had sexual relations with children after they became adults. Ferenczi believed the stories he was getting. It was one thing for adults to fantasize about being molested as children, but quite another to start telling about how they had become molesters themselves.

Ferenczi began to look at the "Oedipal impulse" in a new way. He wondered if the Oedipus complex might be "the result of real acts on the part of adults, namely violent passion directed toward the child, who then develops a fixation, not from desire [as Freud maintained], but from fear."[10] Ferenczi concluded that children are victims of sexual abuse in far greater numbers than anyone suspected. He also wrote: "The obvious objection, that we are dealing with sexual fantasies of the child himself, that is, with hysterical lies, unfortunately is weakened by the multitude of confessions of this kind, on the part of patients in analysis, to assaults on children."[11]

When Ferenczi presented his findings to the Twelfth International Psycho-Analytic Congress in Wiesbaden in 1932, he was accorded the same reception Freud had received more than thirty years earlier: silence and rejection. This time, Freud supported the rejection of Ferenczi's "radical ideas." A few months later Ferenczi died; his ideas died with him.

Thirty years later, by way of the feminist movement, a major challenge was mounted against the degradation of women by psychoanalysts. The psychiatrists' view that a woman was responsible for her sexual attitudes — because of her early sexual fantasies — and for sexual assaults perpetrated on her, made her subject to laws that left her twice a victim: a victim of her attacker and a victim of a legal system that told her she invited the attack. The women's movement also helped society acknowledge that children are being sexually assaulted by their fathers, stepfathers, grandfathers and other trusted adults.

In Canada, people who worked with children tried to determine the dimensions of the problem. Their concern led to the creation of the Committee on Sexual Offences against Children, or the Badgley committee. The committee's report included a 1983 face-to-face survey of two thousand men and women, regarding their sexual experiences as children. The figures startled the committee. By the time she reached the age of seventeen, a woman had a one in four chance of being sexually assaulted in a manner that contravened the Criminal Code of Canada. (One boy in ten was assaulted.)[12]

These figures were similar to figures from the United States.[13] The polls in both countries found that sexual abuse is not a lower-class problem. It cuts right across class boundaries, and is possibly more rampant in middle-class homes than in lower-class homes. (There are more middle-class households in Canada.)

But as reports of sexual abuse mounted, as the allegations piled up, as cases began to go to court, the backlash started. Children lie. How comforting it must be to reinforce the concept of the lying child and the poor accused father. In a world where we need to preserve traditional values, believing the father and denying the child fits right in. One group who would support the father at the expense of the child is called Victims Of Child Abuse Laws (VOCAL). The group's 120 chapters in the United States are composed of men (and a few women) who say they have been falsely accused of sexually abusing children. Other people would like to dismiss the whole problem of sexual abuse as if it were a children's fantasy. Douglas Besharov, at one time director of the National Center on Child Abuse and Neglect, wrote in 1985 that sixty-five percent of the cases of child abuse reported in the United States were unfounded.[14]

What it comes down to is that many of us really do not believe our children. We do not want to accept what is happening to them. We do not want to believe that adults are raping these children, raping them because the children have no power to resist. Many of us have a tough time with it because in the vast majority of cases it's men doing the raping, and men do not like to be reminded of that fact, and would much prefer to cover it up by saying they must protect the innocent father, stepfather, whoever, who has been falsely accused in a custody fight between the parents, or some other situation where a child is being hurt.

Who is doing the hurting? There are different answers to this question, depending on whether the abuse is physical — hitting — or sexual.

Physical abuse occurs mainly in the first years of a child's life, when the child is most vulnerable and most dependent on the parent. One in ten abused kids is abused before his or her first birthday. Half of abused children are six or less. The majority are male. It is generally accepted that most kids are abused in "poor" homes, that is, homes where there is economic stress. (This conclusion is supported by a rise in reported cases of abuse during times of economic hardship.) In Toronto, studies have found that abuse occurs in an environment that is monotonous and lacks stimulation, or where there is a harsh relationship between parent and child characterized by continual verbal abuse, putting down, or excessive authoritarianism.

Popular belief has it that the abused become the abusers, but evidence of this is fragmentary and inconclusive. The police support the belief, and claim that today's abused children become tomorrow's rapists and killers; every police officer can recount stories of criminals who came from deprived, abusing backgrounds. (The backgrounds of men and women serving time suggest the stories are true.)

Figures show that more abuse occurs in single-parent families. (The largest portion of the population living on or below the poverty line is single-parent households headed by females.) The condition of poverty is usually combined with social isolation: the single mother has few or no outside contacts or interests, and feels trapped by the walls of economic duress. In her frustration, she abuses her children. Child welfare agencies describe their "usual client" as single, unemployed, lacking in education and job skills and generally living below the poverty line.[15]

While all these statistics are true, however, there is another side of the story. The poor and the disadvantaged are the users of the social welfare systems. Anyone who has lived in public housing knows well that the knock on the door might be the welfare workers, an inspector, an administrator. There are so many interested parties, all monitoring the family's life. (One woman said, "The only place they don't seem to come is into the bathroom. They certainly come into the bedroom, asking who I am living with.") The middle class is not subjected to the same scrutiny; nor does the middle class use the welfare system. Generally, the middle class has far greater access to support systems and networks; they also have access to legal counsel. (One social worker said, "When you deal with a middle- or upper middle-class family, rest assured in a lot of instances they will tell you to fuck off and talk to their lawyer.")

It is not surprising, then, that figures about abuse are skewed toward the economically disadvantaged. In cases of sexual abuse, the social and economic differences start to blur. Yet it would be wrong not to emphasize the strong correlation between abuse and poverty. Poor families are continually frustrated by their inability to achieve the material standards they see on television. They are crowded into substandard housing; too often, they find half their income devoured by rent. They have to use food banks. They have menial jobs that are both financially and mentally unrewarding. Many are unemployed. Often their children are undernourished, and a child who is undernourished is often unruly and difficult, which further provokes the parents. The harassed mothers do not have the support systems, the money or the contacts to take a break from the children. Not for them a separate room or a baby-sitter.

One social worker said, "If we would only give these people a bit better housing, a bit more cash in their pockets, we could solve a hell of a lot of our caseloads. But it won't happen, because society really believes that these people are undeserving, that they like being poor and living on welfare. My God — they should try it sometime."

Poverty is not the only factor that contributes to abuse. Young women who have been sexually abused and placed in care as children are far more likely to end up as single parents, and these women have a great propensity to become victims of sexual exploitation. They have difficulty establishing a healthy relationship with a man, and suffer depression and anxiety. These young women have children precisely because they need someone to love and to love them. Problems arise when their babies behave as babies — demanding attention, feeding, changing. The demands become insufferable. The return on the emotional investment seems minimal. The child seems to be incapable of obeying or fulfilling the mother's commands, so the child must be punished. That is when the abuse starts.

Defining physical punishment is difficult. A child might end up with a bruise because, after repeated warnings, he or she persists in running out into the street to retrieve a ball. To the parent the hard slap is a last resort, but it seems necessary. If physical punishment is used consistently, though, children begin to learn that those who love them are those who hit. To the children, love and violence become one. In later life, the boy child will transfer that behavior to the marital relationship, or the mother will transfer it to her child.

The profile of the abusing parent includes the unwed teenager mother. Across Canada, a growing number of child mothers are opting to keep their kids. The teenage mom often comes from a low-income family; she possesses few marketable skills and has little education. She is part of the large army of single-parent families who live below the poverty line. These child mothers are ill equipped to take care of their kids. Often they have a low tolerance for frustration; many are impulsive. When the mother's fantasies about the baby and her role as a parent come up against harsh reality, rage, depression, or withdrawal result.

Who becomes a sexual abuser? Here there is no clear pattern. The father who sees his daughter as a substitute wife, the stepfather who has courted the mother to get at the daughter, the grandfather who assaults the granddaughter. They prey on the children, offering nonsexual favors and rewards for sexual favors. Often they offer what the child is lacking: affection. Many girls who are abused become victims because they are isolated, or because they feel unloved and unwanted. In most instances, the offender uses not force but a series of subterfuges or seduction; he involves the child emotionally. His objective is to gain control sexually over his victim, and he sees sexual involvement as a sign that the child accepts and loves him. Most often the child and offender know each other. Sometimes they are related. Usually the relationship goes on over time. The molester can become a trusted and familiar figure in the child's life. It is not unusual for young boys to be victims. Again, the molester uses sexual contact to gain affection and love.

Some people who sexually abuse children use force, verbal threats or violence. To this type of offender, the child is there only to serve his gratification; there is no attempt to gain the child's emotional involvement. The aggression has only one purpose: to accomplish the sexual act. Once that is accomplished, the child is disposable. There is no ongoing relationship. The abuse is an exercise of the power of the adult over the child, and the expression of that power is sexual. While such molesters often do not intend to hurt the child, they do not feel much remorse if they do; a child is an object, and resistance from the child can trigger a violent reaction from the offender. A few molesters take pleasure in attacking children, beating, choking, torturing and then sexually abusing them. Such offenders are punishing the child after planning and fantasizing about the attack. The child becomes the target for the molester's rage and cruelty. These are the offenders who murder. They are at the extreme end of the continuum.

According to those who have studied sexual abuse, a very large number of women who were sexually abused as children wind up marrying child abusers. In some cases the abuse goes on for generations. Social workers are consistently amazed that women who have been abused seem to be able to find an abusing man with ease. These are women who have low self-esteem; they are unlikely to object if they see that their daughters are the victims of abuse.

One other problem worries social workers: the number of teenage girls who, pregnant as the result of sexual abuse, decide to keep their babies. The experts see the pattern repeating itself: the woman perceives herself as a victim, and sets herself up for further victimization. Two facts are known: more than three-quarters of the women doing time in Canada's prisons for women were sexually abused; half the girls who become runaways were also sexually abused.[16]

One inescapable conclusion emerges: society is the abuser of children. Society sets the rules about what is acceptable, what is tolerated, what happens to children. If society does not sanction sexual assault or severe emotional or physical abuse, it does seem willing to tolerate the abuse of children. Society permits children to live in poverty and allows corporal punishment, for example. On the television news we see hundreds of volunteers battling to save a child trapped in a well, yet we allow children to go hungry. We have created a society where kids are less likely to be abused in licenced day-care centers than at home.[17] But then, we don't spend that much on day care, either. As a society, our priorities seem to be based on the immediate — we look for simple solutions to simple problems. We dislike long-term complex problems.

What progress has been made to alleviate the problems of child abuse seems slight indeed. A U.S. survey on family violence undertaken by Professor Straus in 1975 was repeated a decade later. Again parents were asked if they had used violence against their children in the previous year. The study found that, while the overall level of violence remained the same, the most severe forms of punishment had fallen off by forty-seven percent.[18]

Why had this happened? Cynics suggested that people were aware that the results would be made public, and they didn't want to look bad — so they lied the second time around. Some people married later, and more mature parents are perhaps less likely to hit their kids. Many couples were having fewer kids, and fewer kids mean fewer unwanted kids — the usual victims of abuse. In the United States, the National Committee for the Prevention of Child Abuse aimed an advertising campaign at parents who abuse their children. It had a clear, simple message: "Take time out, don't take it out on your kids." Perhaps parents are becoming aware that abusing their children is not acceptable. But in Canada, society is unwilling to launch such a campaign. We will spend millions, and rightly so, to get drunken drivers off the road, but we spend very little to get abusers off the backs of children. We will accept the expenditure of thousands of dollars, even tens of thousands, to provide the finest medical care in the world for a child who needs open-heart surgery or a liver transplant. Yet when it comes to free school lunches or better housing for kids, society is unwilling to make any worthwhile reforms.

Perhaps the payoff seems too remote, too difficult to realize. In 1967, author Jacques Ellul wrote, ''What public opinion does not recognize as fact has no political existence.''[19] That sentence sums up child welfare in Canada. Children do not have a political existence. They are the disenfranchised. Society may stir occasionally to deal with the worst excesses of child abuse, but it will not agree to spend the money or devote resources to change the lot of children, to change the child welfare system, a system designed to protect and act in the child's best interests. One child-care worker summed the situation up: ''What you sees is what you gets, and if you're a kid needing help, what you gets ain't much. All we can try to give them is a little bit of love.''

Epilogue

It was what many parents would call a bloody awful morning, which made it a usual one. As with all schoolday mornings, this one began early, because the twins have to be driven to their high school, a half hour away. (There are no school buses.) To add to the morning misery, the school was overcrowded, so the kids were being taught in shifts, and ours had the morning shift, from eight to one.

Most adults can stagger out into the cold dawn, assemble mind and body, take a shower, dress and go forth to slay the economic dragon. Teenagers are not so built. No way are clothes immediately put on. Color combinations are assembled with the same care that an archaeologist uses to assemble bones. A teenager does not shower; she goes through a ritual that begins with water and ends with makeup. All the while, father (mother was at a conference in Vancouver, giving a paper) was alternating between cajoling, pleading and shouting. The screaming brought the usual — ''You're not in the army anymore, Faz'' (Faz has been my name since they could mumble coherently). Finally, they emerge from the bathroom to kitchen, to eat. Then back for tooth brushing, a last primping and out the door.

We drive down the concession road. It's the ride that gives the kids and me a time to talk about earth-shattering events, free trade, elections, school, math, chemistry, nuclear war and, of course and inevitably, boys. As a male I am supposedly the repository of all wisdom when it comes to boys. Most of the time, we talk about relationships. Teenagers are very astute when it comes to that subject. They have sensitive antennae. They know when others are having a hard time at home, and too often I hear stories about their friends fighting with their parents. Fights my kids say come from a "lack of communication." I hear about kids who love their parents but never talk to them, about parents who never talk to their kids. They talk about gifts becoming a substitute for time, of which I, too, am somewhat guilty. One of my daughters is telling me about a night she spent at one of her girl-friend's homes. "They never talk to each other. Paula doesn't talk to her brother, and she is always fighting with her mom. She loves her mom, but she thinks her mom doesn't listen to her."

None of this is new. All parents have a tendency to tune out. (On occasion, it is a survival mechanism.) But as my children talk, I begin to realize that while we may love our children, very often we do not like them. They are an encumbrance, a financial and emotional drain we are often unprepared for. I remember a joke one of my colleagues told me. "When do people start living? When the dog dies and the kids leave home."

A recent survey asked women when they were happiest, and most of them replied, when they were living with someone or single. They were least happy when married with children, but happiness returned when the kids were gone. A friend of mine who works on Bay Street summed it up: "I would not recommend kids as an investment. Who would invest the $250,000 it takes to raise the kid through to university, suffer the emotional strain, worrying about everything from drugs to school marks, then watch the investment walk out the door with a merry goodbye, never knowing if they will repay what you have put in? I suppose if they have kids, you become a grandparent. But what is the payoff? Why do it? I'll tell you why — because in the end you sort of love them, you get a kick out of their achievements, you cry with them. You relive your own life, and hope they do a better job. I would not have had any gerbils, cats, dogs or rabbits otherwise. I would not owe the bank either, I guess.''

The other payoff is the real joy you can get out of liking your kids. Too many parents love but don't like their kids. I like mine, I enjoy being with them, talking, going to the movies, having dinner with them. I am lucky. And I'm equally lucky in having a wife who has one basic rule: listen to what they are saying and treat them like people. But the main lesson was to make sure they know you love them, that no matter what, you are in their corner, on their side. Feeling it is not enough; you have to show them and tell them that you care. So far, it seems to have worked.

My profound thoughts are disturbed by my daughters asking me a question about Canadian history. Just before we get to the school, Alexis says that she has invited one of her friends to sleep over. I ask who and when. I pull up at the entrance and they get out. ''You know, Faz, I love you and Mum. You give us our freedom. I can ask people to stay over and you just accept it. Other parents don't do that.'' And off they go. Sure we do, because we love and trust you. All it takes is a little bit of love.

Notes

Introduction

1. Joseph Goldstein, Anna Freud and Albert Solnit *Before the Best Interests of the Child* (New York: Free Press, 1973), p.91.
2. R.D. Laing, *The Politics of the Family* (Toronto: CBC, 1968), pp. 3–7.
3. Laing, *Politics*, pp 30–31.

Chapter 1

1. These studies include Mark David Janus, A. McCormack, A.W. Burgess and C. Hartman, *Adolescent Runaways, Causes and Consequences* (Lexington, Mass.: Lexington Books, 1987); ''Kids Who Run: A Forum on Repetitive Runaways,'' held in Toronto on March 3 and 4, 1988; Ruth Heron, ''Runaway Children: A Police Perspective,'' a paper presented to Covenant House's symposium on street youth, held in Toronto on November 2, 3 and 4, 1987; *Facts on Runaway Youth* (Washington, D.C.: National Youth Network Alliance, 1985); and *To Whom Do They Belong? A Profile of America's Runaway Youth and the Programs to Help Them* (Washington, D.C.: National Network of Runaway Youth Services, 1985).
2. I looked at eight documents in particular. One was a report called ''Outreach and Rehabilitation Services to Prostitutes and Youth on the Street,''

which was presented by Toronto's Neighbour-
hoods Committee to the City's Planning Department in 1983. In the summer of 1987, Canada's
National Youth in Care Network in Ottawa published a paper called "On the Other Side," com-
prising comments from young people about
working on the streets. F. Mathews presented a
discussion paper on child prostitution to the
National Consultation on Adolescent Prostitutes.
The paper, whose title I have been unable to locate,
was published by Ottawa's Child Welfare Association in 1987. Mathews also wrote a book, *Familiar
Strangers: A Study of Adolescent Prostitution*, which
was published in Toronto in 1987 by Central
Toronto Youth Services. A useful article, "Sexual
Abuse: an Antecedent to Prostitution," was written by M.H. Silbert and A.M. Pines and appeared
in *Child Abuse and Neglect*, vol. 5, no. 4, 1981, pp.
407–411. A good book is D. Finkelhor's *Sexually Vic-
timized Children* (New York: Free Press, 1979). In
1985, Ontario's Ministry of Community and Social
Services published M. Benjamin's "Juvenile Prostitution: A Portrait of 'The Life.'" And finally, I read
Kelly Toughill, "A Tale of Self-Destruction,"
Toronto *Star*, October 18, 1988.

3. This figure was quoted in Patricia Hersch, "Coming of Age in City Streets," in *Psychology Today*,
vol. 22, January 1988, p. 31.

4. The study was carried out by Covenant House in
1987-88.

5. Jacqueline Swartz, "Runaways Often Sexually
Abused," *CMAJ*, vol. 134, April 1986, pp. 944–948.

6. The information is cited by the Badgeley Report
Committee in *Sexual Offences Against Children*, their

report presented to the Minister of Justice and the Minister of Health and Welfare (published in Ottawa in two volumes in 1984).

7. These statistics were presented to me by Professor Chris Bagley, Faculty of Social Welfare, Univ. of Calgary, in an interview during the summer of 1988.

Chapter 2

1. Nancy Pamenter-Potvin, "Physical Abuse," in *Child Abuse and Neglect Law*, ed. Douglas J. Besharov (Washington, D.C.: Child Welfare League of America, 1985). Pamenter-Potvin is quoting Juvenile Court Judge Peter Leveque.

Section 43 confirms in our law what was common practice in British jurisprudence, which goes back to 1860. At that time Britain's Chief Justice Cockburn summed up a case involving an assault on a child by a teacher: "By the law of England, a parent or schoolmaster, who for this purpose represents the parent, and has the parental authority delegated to him, may for the purpose of correcting what is evil in the child, inflict moderate and reasonable corporal punishment, always however, with this condition, that it be moderate and reasonable." (H.T.G. Andrews, ed., *Family Law in the Family Courts*, Toronto: Carswell, 1973). See also Corinne Robertshaw, "Prevention, Programming and Child Abuse," in *Community Mental Health Action*, ed. D. Paul Lumsden (Ottawa: Canadian Mental Health Association, 1984), pp. 96–98.

See also various cases from our courts, in which force was deemed reasonable. For example, *The King v. Zink* (1910) 18, CCC 456; *Rex v. Metcalfe* (1927) 49, CCC 290; *Regina v. Haberstock* (1970) 1, CCC (2d) 43; *La Reine c. Matieux* (1972) R.L. 526. See also *The Child at Risk,* a report of the Standing Senate Committee on Health, Welfare and Science (Ottawa: Supply and Services, 1980), p. 54; and D.C. Dutton, ''Evidence Submitted to the House of Commons Standing Committee on Health, Welfare and Social Affairs, Respecting Inquiry into Violence in the Family,'' *Proceedings*, February 4, 1982, pp. 25–26. (The evidence was presented because of the ''joke'' in the House of Commons about wife battering.)

2. The quote is from the Talmud. See Will Durant, *The Age of Faith*, vol. 4 of his *History of Civilization* (New York: Simon and Schuster, 1950), p. 360.

3. Anne Russell, ''The Emancipation of Children,'' a paper given at the Annual Conference of the Alberta Psychological Association, in October 1974. The conference papers were published; this quotation is from p. 10.

4. Rafael Sajan, ''Introduction to the Law of Minors,'' in *Proceedings of the Eighth Congress of the International Association of Youth Magistrates* (Geneva: UNESCO, 1970), p. 25.

5. C.C. Coultin, *Life in the Middle Ages* (Cambridge: Cambridge University Press, 1930), vol. 3, p. 114. See also his *Five Centuries of Religion* (Cambridge: Cambridge University Press, 1923), vol. 1, p. 174.

6. Fernand Braudel, *The Structures of Everyday Life* (New York: Harper and Row, 1979), vol. 1, p. 491.

7. Desmond Morton and Terry Copp, *Working People* (Ottawa: Deneau and Greenberg, 1980), pp. 30, 61, 84–85.

8. Elizabeth Pleck, *Domestic Tyranny: The Making of Social Policy Against Family Violence From Colonial Times to the Present* (New York: Oxford Univ. Press, 1987).

9. Joseph Goldstein, Anna Freud and Albert Solnit, *Before the Best Interests of the Child* (New York: Free Press, 1973). See also S.D. Clark, *Social Development in Canada* (Toronto: Univ. of Toronto Press, 1942).

10. The commission was quoted in Corinne Robertshaw, "Child Protection in Canada" (Ottawa: Health and Welfare Canada, 1981).

11. *Child Abuse and Neglect,* a report for the House of Commons prepared by the Standing Committee on Health, Welfare and Social Affairs (Ottawa: Health and Welfare Canada, 1976), p. 20.

12. Brian Fraser, "Legal Rights of Children," a paper presented to the Symposium on the Battered Child, held in Denver, Colorado, May 31 to June 1, 1973.

13. D.J. MacDougall, "Children's Rights: An Evaluation of the Controversy," in *The Challenge of Child Welfare,* ed. L. Levitt and B. Wharf (Vancouver: UBC Press, 1985), pp. 266–275.

Chapter 3

1. Justice T.G. Zuber, *Report on the Ontario Courts of Inquiry* (Toronto: Attorney General of Ontario, 1987), p. 63.

2. Zuber, *Report*, p. 67.

3. Zuber, *Report*, p. 97.
4. K. Marron explains what judges go through in *Ritual Abuse: Canada's Most Infamous Trial on Child Abuse* (Toronto: Seal, 1988), pp. 243–249.

Chapter 4

1. Brian Raychaba, *A Report on the Special Needs of Youth in the Care of the Child Welfare System* (Ottawa: National Youth in Care Network, 1987), p. 7.
2. Sally Palmer, *Children in Long Term Care* (New York: Department of Health and Welfare, Project 555-36-4, 1976).
3. The information is from a report called *Emergency Shelters for Youth* (Toronto: Social Planning Council of Metro Toronto, 1988), pp. 8–10.
4. The results of the poll were published as *A New Statistical Perspective on Youth in Canada* (Toronto: Gallup, 1984), p. 6.
5. Sue Hebb, "Youth in Care Tell About Their Needs," Digby *Courier*, 20 May 1987.
6. H. Philip Hepworth, "Child Neglect and Abuse," in *Challenge of Child Welfare*, ed. L. Levitt and B. Wharf (Vancouver: UBC Press, 1985).
7. Diana Coulter, "Government Wards Set Adrift at Age 18 Face Hard, Lonely Life on Streets," Edmonton *Journal*, 13 July 1987.
8. Steve McNeill, "Life in an Institution Can Be Terrifying," Hamilton *Spectator*, 15 May 1986.

Chapter 5

1. Marilyn Callahan, "Public Apathy and Government Parsimony: A Review of Child Welfare in

Canada," in *Challenge of Child Welfare*, ed. L. Levitt and B. Wharf (Vancouver: UBC Press, 1985), p. 18.

2. Robert McFadden, ''An Investigation of Burnout Among Front Line Child Protection Workers,'' an unpublished Ph.D. thesis for the University of Toronto. McFadden was quoted in a submission to John Sweeney, Minister of Community and Social Services, on behalf of unionized children's aid society workers on June 15, 1987. The submission was published; the McFadden quotation appears on p. 11.

3. Michael Benjamin, ''The Organization and Structure of the Child Protective Services in Metropolitan Toronto,'' an unpublished Ph.D. thesis for the University of Toronto, 1986, p. 95.

4. Lawrence Shulman, ''The Dynamics of Child Welfare,'' in *Challenge*.

Chapter 6

1. Darnell Consulting Inc., for the Ontario Association of Children's Aid Societies' Residential Care Research Project, ''The Future of Foster Care'' (Toronto: OACAS, January 1988), pp. 77–85. Market Facts of Canada, ''Foster Care in Ontario, A Market Research Study, Stages 1 and 2'' (Toronto: Ministry of Community and Social Services, 1981), pp. 29–30. H. Philip Hepworth, ''Substitute Care: The Range of Responses,'' in *The Challenge of Child Welfare*, ed. L. Levitt and B. Wharf (Vancouver: UBC Press, 1985), pp. 142–153.

2. The report, called ''Foster Care Training: A Comprehensive Approach,'' was prepared and published by the British Columbia Federation of Foster

Parents Associations in 1987. The profile appears on pp. 16–18.

3. Peter Silverman, *Who Speaks for the Children?* (Toronto: Musson, 1978), pp. 150–151.

4. The quotation is from Darnell's research project, "The Future of Foster Care," p. 259.

5. The study, *An Analysis of Foster Care Practices in Ontario*, was done by the Levy-Coughlin Partnership (Toronto: Ministry of Community and Social Services, 1984), pp. 65–91.

6. The study is Darnell's research project; information about support is on pp. 211–215.

7. The questions are asked in Darnell's research project.

8. Margaret Polanyi, "Probe Ordered Into Complaint Against Home," Toronto *Globe and Mail*, 14 August 1987.

Chapter 7

1. Celeste Durant, in an article titled "Violence Wracks the Home," published in the Toronto *Star*, 14 May 1979, quotes Richard Gelles, Associate Professor of Sociology and Anthropology, University of Rhode Island.

2. The study is described in Richard Gelles, Murray Straus and Susanne Steinmetz, *Behind Closed Doors: Violence in American Family Life* (New York: Anchor Press, 1980).

3. Ambroise Tardieu, quoted in Jeffrey Masson, *The Assault on Truth: Freud's Suppression of the Seduction Theory* (New York: Farrar, Straus and Giroux, 1984), pp. 18–19.

4. John Caffey, "Multiple Fractures in the Long Bones

of Infants Suffering From Chronic Subdural Hematoma," in *American Journal of Roentgenology, Radium Therapy and Nuclear Medicine*, vol. 56, 1946, pp. 163–173.

5. Frederic Silverman, "The Roentgen Manifestation of Unrecognized Skeletal Trauma in Infants," in *American Journal of Roentgenology*, vol. 69, 1953, pp. 413–426.

6. Tardieu, quoted in Masson, *Assault*, p. 23.

7. Alfred Fournier, quoted in Masson, *Assault*, p. 44.

8. John Crewdson, *By Silence Betrayed* (Toronto: Little, Brown, 1988), p. 37.

9. Sigmund Freud, quoted in Masson, *Assault*, pp. 108–110.

10. Sandor Ferenczi, quoted in Masson, *Assault*, p. 147.

11. Ferenczi, in Masson, p. 148.

12. The numbers are cited by the Badgeley Report Committee in *Sexual Offences Against Children*, a report presented to the ministers of Justice and Health and published in Ottawa in 1984. Numbers appear on pp. 179, 180–182, 219, 1061, and Table 6.1. See also C. Bagley, "Child Abuse, a Child Welfare Perspective," in *The Challenge of Child Welfare*, ed. L. Levitt and B. Wharf (Vancouver: UBC Press, 1985), pp. 66–89.

13. The U.S. figures come from a Los Angeles *Times* poll, quoted in Crewdson, *By Silence Betrayed*, p. 28. See also Florence Rush, *The Best Kept Secret: Sexual Abuse of Children* (Englewood Cliffs, N.J.: Prentice-Hall Inc., 1980).

14. Besharov's thoughts are cited in Crewdson, *By Silence Betrayed*, p. 36.

15. M. Martin, "Poverty and Child Welfare," in *Challenge*, pp. 53–64. The client is described on p. 55. See also *In the Best Interests of the Child* (Ottawa: the National Council of Welfare, 1979), particularly p. 2. Also, the Metro Toronto Catholic Children's Aid Society published a fact sheet, called "Profile of Our Clients," in February 1987.

16. Numbers come from social workers who deal with women behind bars. See also Sara Jane Growe, "Little Mothers," Toronto *Star*, 17 June 1987; and H. Philip Hepworth, "Child Neglect and Abuse," in *Challenge*, p. 38.

17. Ann Rauhala, "Risk of Abuse Lower in Day Care, Study Finds," Toronto *Globe and Mail*, 23 March 1988.

18. Crewdson, *By Silence Betrayed*, p. 233.

19. Jacques Ellul, *The Political Illusion* (New York: Knopf, 1967), p. 75.